MY FIRST BRITANNICA

Asia, Australia, and New Zealand

7

ENCYCLOPÆDIA
Britannica®

CHICAGO   LONDON   NEW DELHI   PARIS   SEOUL   SYDNEY   TAIPEI   TOKYO

© 2004 by Encyclopædia Britannica, Inc.

International Standard Book Number: 1-59339-048-3 (set)
International Standard Book Number: 1-59339-055-6 (volume 7)

No part of this work may be reproduced or utilized in any form or by any means, electronic or mechanical, including photocopying, recording, or by any information storage and retrieval system, without permission in writing from the publisher. Printed in Singapore.

My First Britannica:
Volume 7: Asia, Australia, and New Zealand 2004

Britannica.com may be accessed on the Internet at http://www.britannica.com.

Encyclopædia Britannica, Britannica, and the Thistle logo are registered trademarks of Encyclopædia Britannica, Inc.

Asia, Australia, and New Zealand

TABLE OF CONTENTS

INTRODUCTION 5

Asia

Asia: The Largest Continent 6

East Asia

China: Asia's Largest Country 8

  Beijing, China: Home of the Forbidden City 10

  The Great Wall: Ancient China's Giant Guardian 12

Japan: Volcanoes, Earthquakes, and Plum Rains 14

  Japan: Modern Nation of Ancient Traditions 16

Korean Peninsula: An Asian Land Divided 18

  Pyongyang, North Korea:

    North Korea's Age-Old Capital 20

  Seoul, South Korea: A Modern Ancient Capital 22

Southeast Asia

Phnom Penh, Cambodia: The City of Lady Penh 24

  Angkor Wat: Cambodia's Treasured Temple 26

Indonesia: Island Nation of Southeast Asia 28

Yangon, Myanmar: City of the Gold Pagoda 30

Philippines: Tropical Island Republic 32

Singapore: The Lion City 34

Thailand: Kingdom of Southeast Asia 36

  Bangkok, Thailand: City of Angels 38

Vietnam: North and South 40

  Hanoi, Vietnam: Capital of Reunited Vietnam 42

South Asia

Afghanistan: Mountain Country 44

Bangladesh: Land of the Bengals 46

Thimphu, Bhutan: City in the Heart of the Himalayas . . . 48

India: Land of Temples and Shrines 50

  Taj Mahal: Wonder of the World 52

Nepal: Country of Mount Everest 54

  Kathmandu, Nepal: City of Palaces 56

Pakistan: A Young Country with an Ancient History 58

  Pakistan: Land of the Indus Civilization 60

Sri Lanka: Island Nation of Natural Riches 62

The Middle East and Transcaucasia

Fertile Crescent: Cradle of Civilization 64

Yerevan, Armenia: City of Cafés 66

Istanbul, Turkey: City on Two Continents 68

Iran: Modern Persia 70

Baghdad, Iraq: City of Arabian Nights 72

Israel: The Jewish State 74

  Jerusalem: Holy City 76

Amman, Jordan: City on Seven Hills 78

Beirut, Lebanon: The City of Wells 80

Oman: Rocky Soils and Petroleum Riches 82

Mecca, Saudi Arabia: Holiest City of Islam 84

Damascus, Syria: Pearl of the East 86

Australia and New Zealand

AUSTRALIA

Australia: Island Continent 88

  Canberra, Australia: Meeting Place on a Hill 90

  Great Barrier Reef: Island of Reefs Within Reefs 92

  Sydney, Australia: A Magnificent Harbour City 94

  Western Australia: Desert State 96

NEW ZEALAND

New Zealand: Land of the Long White Cloud 98

  Wellington, New Zealand:

    A Visit to New Zealand's Capital 100

GLOSSARY 103

Asia, Australia, and New Zealand

I N T R O D U C T I O N

How did the Forbidden City get its name?

What is the holiest city of Islam? Who built the Taj Mahal?

Where is the largest coral reef in the world?

In Volume 7, *Asia, Australia, and New Zealand,* you'll discover answers to these questions and many more. Through pictures, articles, and fun facts, you'll learn about the people, traditions, landscapes, and history that make up many of the countries and cities of Asia, Australia, and New Zealand.

To help you on your journey, we've provided the following signposts in *Asia, Australia, and New Zealand*:

■ **Subject Tabs**—The coloured box in the upper corner of each right-hand page will quickly tell you the article subject.

■ **Search Lights**—Try these mini-quizzes before and after you read the article and see how much - *and how quickly* - you can learn. You can even make this a game with a reading partner. (Answers are upside down at the bottom of one of the pages.)

■ **Did You Know?**—Check out these fun facts about the article subject. With these surprising 'factoids', you can entertain your friends, impress your teachers, and amaze your parents.

■ **Picture Captions**—Read the captions that go with the photos. They provide useful information about the article subject.

■ **Vocabulary**—New or difficult words are in **bold type**. You'll find them explained in the Glossary at the back of this volume. And there's a complete listing of all Glossary terms in the set in the *Reference Guide and Index*, Volume 13.

■ **Learn More!**—Follow these pointers to related articles throughout the set.

■ **Maps**—You'll find lots of information in this volume's many maps.

■ The **Country Maps** point out national capitals. **Globes** beside Subject Tabs show where countries are located in the world.

■ The **Continent Maps** have a number key showing the location of all countries.

■ The **Icons** on the maps highlight major geographic features and climate. Here's a key to what the map icons mean:

☀ Deserts and Other Dry Areas 　 🌴 Rainforests

❄ Polar Regions and Other Frozen Areas 　 🌳 General Forests

⛰ Mountains

■ The **Mini-Atlas**, found in Volume 13, offers detailed maps, useful data tables, and assorted photographs of each continent.

And don't forget: If you're not sure where to start, where you saw something before, or where to go next, the ***Reference Guide and Index*** (Volume 13) will point the way.

The Great Wall of China
© Keren Su/Corbis

Have a great trip!

MY FIRST BRITANNICA

True or false?
The highest point on Earth is in Asia.

43

11

2

3

23

16

39

18

15

20

4

33

45

35

30

48

14

1

31

19

46

44

41

21

26

28

12

6

5

27

22

47

9

42

8

34

7

24

36

38

25

13

Statue of Buddha in Si Satchanalai, Thailand.
© Royalty-Free/Corbis

DID YOU KNOW?
Asia is the birthplace of all the major religions of the world.

The Largest Continent

Asia is the world's largest continent. It covers about one-third of the Earth's land and has about three-fifths of the world's population. Japan, China, India, and Taiwan are some of the most familiar of Asia's nearly 50 countries. In fact, Asia is so big that it's often easier to talk about the **regions** rather than the countries of Asia. The region names commonly used are North Asia, Central Asia, East Asia, Southeast Asia, South Asia, and South-west Asia (the last is one usually called the Middle East).

Most of the continent is made up of mountains and **tablelands**. The Himalayan mountain chain in South Asia includes the highest point on Earth, Mount Everest. The Earth's lowest point, the Dead Sea, is in Asia too.

Asia is home to many kinds of animals. Reindeer, Arctic foxes and hares, seals, walruses, and lemmings can be found in the far north. Elk, brown bears, and sables live in the cool forests. Antelope, wild sheep, and goats are found in the **steppes** and deserts. Black bears, pandas, tigers, and monkeys can be found in southern and eastern Asia. Southern Asia is also noted for elephants, leopards, crocodiles, cobras, and peacocks.

Northern Asia has very cold winters and cool summers. It is covered by tundra - vast treeless plains common in cold regions. Central Asia has cold winters and hot summers with little rainfall. Southern Asia has a warm climate all year, with a lot of rain. There are rainforests all across southern Asia. And nearly all Asian countries share one very important food plant: rice.

LEARN MORE! READ THESE ARTICLES...
CONTINENTS (VOLUME 1) • EUROPE (VOLUME 6)
MOUNTAINS (VOLUME 1)

29 17 37 40 32 13 10

COUNTRIES OF ASIA

1. Afghanistan
2. Armenia
3. Azerbaijan
4. Bahrain
5. Bangladesh
6. Bhutan
7. Brunei
8. Cambodia
9. China
10. East Timor
11. Georgia
12. India
13. Indonesia
14. Iran
15. Iraq
16. Israel
17. Japan
18. Jordan
19. Kazakhstan
20. Kuwait
21. Kyrgyzstan
22. Laos
23. Lebanon
24. Malaysia
25. Maldives
26. Mongolia
27. Myanmar
28. Nepal
29. North Korea
30. Oman
31. Pakistan
32. Philippines
33. Qatar
34. Russia (part)
35. Saudi Arabia
36. Singapore
37. South Korea
38. Sri Lanka
39. Syria
40. Taiwan
41. Tajikistan
42. Thailand
43. Turkey
44. Turkmenistan
45. United Arab Emirates
46. Uzbekistan
47. Vietnam
48. Yemen

Answer: TRUE. The world's tallest mountain, Mount Everest, is in Asia.

Asia's Largest Country

The People's Republic of China is Asia's largest country and has more people than any other country in the world - more than a billion and a quarter! The capital city is Beijing. Han (or Mandarin) is the most widely spoken language of China's several dozen languages. The Chinese civilization is one of the world's oldest and has produced such famous thinkers as Confucius.

Parts of China are very mountainous, as is the **Plateau** of Tibet in south-western China. One part of the plateau is called 'the Roof of the World'. China is so big that some parts are scorching hot deserts while it rains almost every day in some south-eastern regions. Many boats and ships carry people and goods on China's major rivers - the Huang He, Yangtze, and Xi. China also has many railroads as well as three of the world's longest highways.

China's enormous and varied land area supports many plants and animals. Some Chinese animals have become **extinct** in the rest of the world, including the giant salamander, the giant panda, and the great paddlefish. Many of China's trees provide useful substances. The tung tree and the camphor tree produce valuable oils. The lacquer (or varnish) tree produces substances used in making wooden objects. And from the star anise tree comes a food flavouring. In addition, Chinese farmers produce more rice than does any other country.

People around the world enjoy eating Chinese food. But China has many more traditional and **regional** dishes than most non-Chinese know about. In addition to rice and noodles, Chinese dishes include delicacies such as steamed chicken feet and hundred-year-old eggs.

LEARN MORE! READ THESE ARTICLES...
CONFUCIUS (VOLUME 5) • MAO ZEDONG (VOLUME 4)
PANDAS (VOLUME 12)

SEARCH LIGHT

Find and correct the mistake in the following sentence: The People's Republic of China is the largest country in Asia and has the most people: more than a million and a quarter.

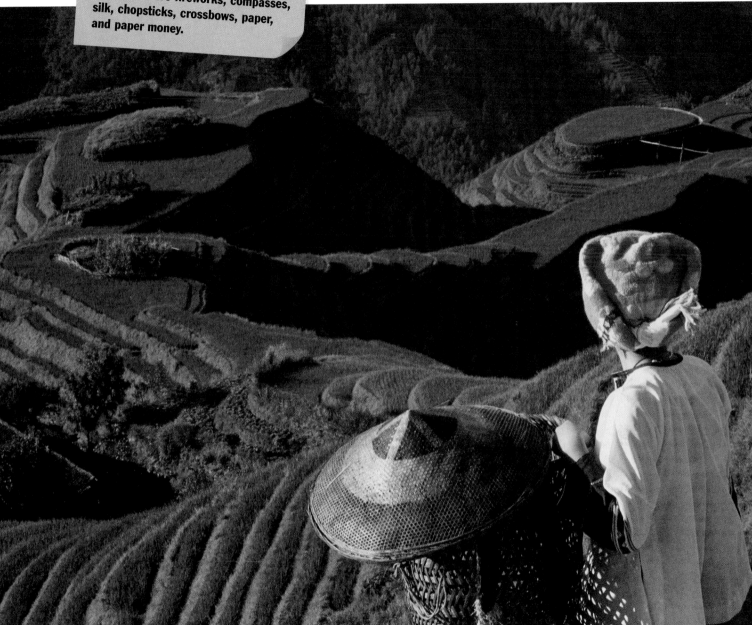

Rice is one of the most important crops grown in China. Farmers use terraced fields such as these to grow rice on hillsides.
© Keren Su/Corbis

Answer: The People's Republic of China is the largest country in Asia and has the most people in the world: more than a billion and a quarter.

Many people in Beijing use bicycles to get from place to place.
© Joseph Sohm—ChromoSohm Inc./Corbis

DID YOU KNOW?
The Forbidden City was well named. The 'common people' were never allowed in. Even those who were allowed in, such as the emperor's family, could go into only certain parts of the city.

Home of the Forbidden City

Beijing is the capital of the People's Republic of China. For many years the city was known by English speakers as Peking. China used to be ruled by emperors, and Beijing was the home of those emperors. Their palaces were located in an area that is called the Forbidden City because common people were not allowed inside. The Forbidden City is now a museum.

Next to the Forbidden City is Tiananmen Square. It is one of the largest public squares in the world. Beijing is also famous for its parks.

The Forbidden City, in Beijing, China.
© Keren Su/Corbis

Zhongshan Park is located in the heart of the city. It holds the **Altar** of Earth and Harvests, where the emperor made offerings to the gods of earth and farming. Beihai Park has a big lake and several artificial hills and islands. On top of one of the hills stands the beautiful White **Pagoda**. In summer the lake is full of rowboats. In winter it freezes, and people use it as an ice skating rink.

The Beijing Zoo was once called the Garden of Ten Thousand Animals. It doesn't really have that many animals, but it does have lots of interesting ones, including some famous giant pandas. Of course, there are places to visit outside the parks. Some people like to tour the neighbourhoods of the city. The city has many narrow alleys, or *hutongs*. Old houses with enclosed courtyards and tiny gardens of potted plants open off the alleys.

There's much to see in Beijing. And, especially exciting, the Olympics will be held there in 2008.

LEARN MORE! READ THESE ARTICLES...
CHINA (VOLUME 7)
A CHINESE CINDERELLA STORY: YEH-SHEN (VOLUME 5)
EMPRESS OF CHINA (VOLUME 4)

SEARCH LIGHT

Find and correct the mistake in the following sentence: The city of Beijing has many lovely parks, or *hutongs*.

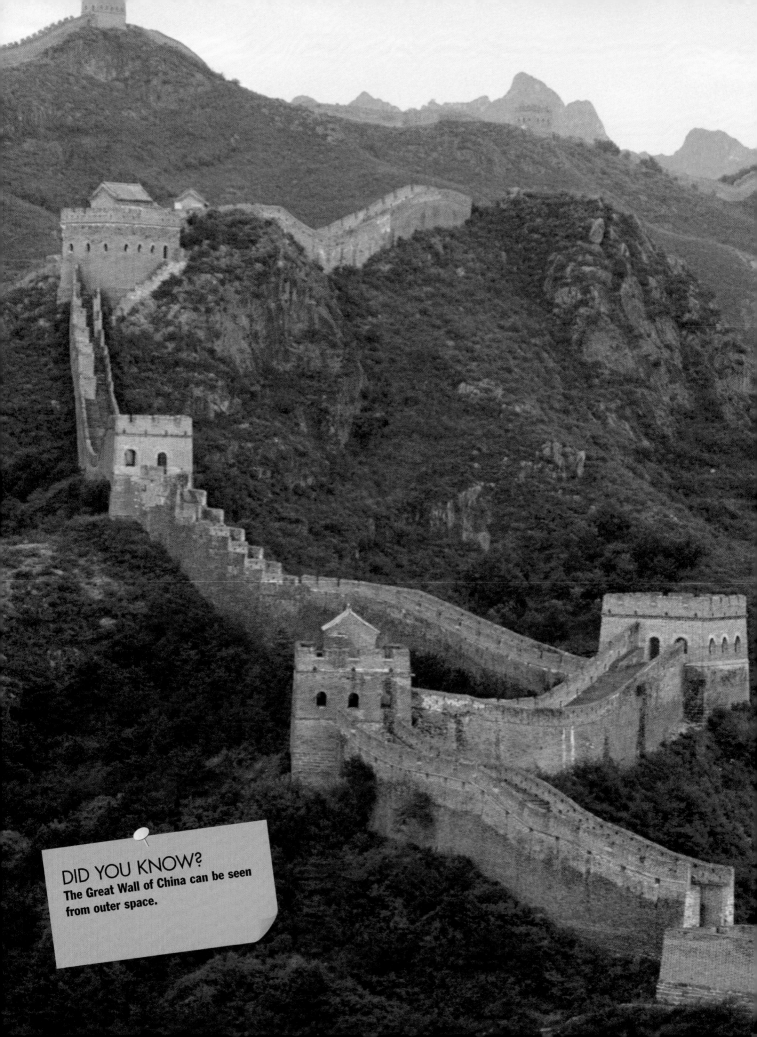

DID YOU KNOW?
The Great Wall of China can be seen from outer space.

Ancient China's
Giant Guardian

SEARCH LIGHT

The Great Wall of China is the largest structure humans have ever built. Chinese **emperors** had the wall built to guard the country from raids or invasions. It runs from east to west for more than 6,400 kilometres as it stretches across the mountains and valleys of northern China. It is about 6 metres thick at its base and as tall as a house. The entire wall is made of earth and

Why did the Chinese emperors have the Great Wall built?

Tourists visiting the Great Wall of China.
© Dean Conger/Corbis

stones. The wall also had watchtowers placed along its length.

Different parts of the wall were built at different times, but all of it was finished long before there were machines to help with the building. Thousands of men worked to build the wall. Many of them died while working on it.

After the Great Wall was built, the people of China felt safer. If an enemy approached the wall, smoke signals would be passed from watchtower to watchtower. A signal fire would be lighted if an attack came at night. An alarm would be sounded, and the emperor's army would rush to defend the wall.

But the Great Wall didn't always provide protection. Because the wall was so long, some parts of it were guarded better than others. Sometimes enemies broke through. Finally, the Chinese stopped depending on their wall.

Today the Great Wall is a great attraction for visitors to China. In 1987, UNESCO (the United Nations Educational, Scientific, and Cultural Organization) named the Great Wall a World Heritage site.

LEARN MORE! READ THESE ARTICLES...
ANGKOR WAT (VOLUME 7) • CHINA (VOLUME 7) • EGYPT (VOLUME 8)

The Great Wall of China is one of the most remarkable structures on Earth. It is more than 6,400 kilometres long and is one of the largest construction projects ever carried out. Work on parts of the wall began more than 2,500 years ago.
© Keren Su/Corbis

Volcanoes, Earthquakes, and Plum Rains

 Japan is made up of a string of islands that stretches for about 2,400 kilometres along the coast of north-eastern Asia in the Pacific Ocean. The four main islands are Honshu, Hokkaido, Kyushu, and Shikoku. The largest of them is Honshu.

Most of the islands are covered with hills and mountains. Many of the mountains are volcanoes. Some of them are active, and some are 'asleep'. Mount Fuji is a sleeping, or dormant, volcano. It is Japan's highest mountain, reaching a height of 3,776 metres. Rivers flowing past the volcanoes get so much **acid** in them that they can't be used to water crops.

There are many lush forests in Japan. Japanese cherry trees, famous for their spring blossoms, are planted throughout the country. The forests stay beautifully green because it rains and snows so much in Japan. Most parts of the country get more than 100 centimetres of rain each year. The summer rains are called *baiu*, which means 'plum rain'. They are called that because they begin at the time when the plums ripen. Some parts of Japan get many centimetres of snow each winter.

Many kinds of wild animal can be found in Japan's forested areas. These animals include bears, badgers, otters, mink, deer, and foxes.

Tokyo

DID YOU KNOW?
Mount Fuji may not seem so high compared with some of the world's other mountains. But it's high enough that during the summer the temperature at the top is 22°C cooler than it is at the bottom.

Mount Fuji is considered the sacred symbol of Japan. It's actually a volcano, but it hasn't erupted since 1707. On the right is a pagoda, a kind of tower with curving roofs at each storey.
© Jose Fuste Raga/Corbis

Japan has many **wildlife sanctuaries** to protect all these wonderful creatures.

Did you know that there are about 1,000 earth tremors in Japan every year? Fortunately, most are not very strong, though violent earthquakes do occur sometimes. When that happens, there is a danger of tsunamis, giant tidal waves along the coasts.

LEARN MORE! READ THESE ARTICLES...
- JAPAN: MODERN NATION OF ANCIENT TRADITIONS (VOLUME 7)
- KOREAN PENINSULA (VOLUME 7)
- TSUNAMIS (VOLUME 1)

SEARCH LIGHT

The largest island in Japan is
a) Honshu.
b) Kyushu.
c) Hokkaido.

Answer: a) Honshu.

Modern Nation
of Ancient Traditions

When you're in Japan, you'll notice something that is really striking: the mixture of old things and new. On the one hand, you'll see beautiful old **pagodas** and **shrines**. On the other hand, you'll find skyscrapers, overpasses, and underground trains.

Some people in Japan continue to fish for a living, just as their ancestors had for thousands of years. Salmon, sardines, tuna, squid, mackerel, cod, and mullet are the important fish they catch. The Japanese people catch more than 5 million tonnes of fish each year. This makes Japan one of the world's leading fishing nations.

Skyscrapers in Shinjuku, a main shopping district in Tokyo.
© Jose Fuste Raga/Corbis

But Japan is also one of the most developed countries in the world. It is one of the world's biggest producers of motorcars, computers, cameras, radio and television sets, watches, microwave ovens, and many more electronic items.

Tokyo, Japan's capital, is one of the world's largest cities. It has many skyscrapers and grand shopping centres and is similar in some ways to New York City. The busy Ginza shopping area is often referred to as Tokyo's Fifth Avenue. But you will also find many Buddhist temples and shrines scattered throughout the city, and they are quiet and peaceful.

The traditional court music of Japan is called *gagaku* and can be heard in Tokyo. But so can a lot of Western music, such as jazz, rock, and blues. And all the latest pop songs that you would hear in English-speaking countries can be heard in Tokyo too.

This mix of ancient and modern culture makes Japan an exciting place to live or visit.

LEARN MORE! READ THESE ARTICLES...
BASHO (VOLUME 3) • HIROHITO (VOLUME 4)
JAPAN: VOLCANOES, EARTHQUAKES, AND PLUM RAINS (VOLUME 7)

SEARCH LIGHT

Are each of the following things part of old Japan or new Japan?
- shrines
- skyscrapers
- underground trains
- *gagaku*
- rock and jazz
- fishing

DID YOU KNOW?

Shinjuku train station in Tokyo is perhaps the busiest train station in the world. About 2 million people pass through it every day.

Built in the 7th century, Senso Temple is the oldest of Tokyo's many Buddhist temples.
© Richard T. Nowitz/Corbis

Answer: Shrines, *gagaku* (court music), and fishing have all been part of Japan for many hundreds of years. Skyscrapers, underground trains, and rock and jazz music are all fairly new to Japan.

열 더 민 군 청 천 기 년 대

MONUMENT DEDICATED TO
THE PHILIPPINE ARMED FORCES IN THE KOREAN WAR

DID YOU KNOW?

For many Koreans the number 4 is considered unlucky, just as the number 13 is for some Westerners. Four is unlucky because in Korean it is pronounced the same as the word for 'death'.

An Asian Land Divided

North Korea

South Korea

The Korean **peninsula** is a land of beautiful mountains. For a long time it was a single country. Today it is divided into two countries - North Korea and South Korea. But though they are separate, they share a border and a common history that stretches back thousands of years.

Korea has a rich culture that was influenced by China, especially in early times. The Buddhist and Confucian religions came to Korea from China. Over the years, however, Korea developed a culture that is very much its own. For example, even though it once used the Chinese system of writing, the Korean language isn't closely related to any other language. And Korean music sounds quite different from other East Asian music. In the folk music called *p'ansori*, a singer-storyteller performs with a drummer. In dance and other music, the *kayagum*, a stringed instrument, is an original Korean favourite. Many people around the world love to eat Korean food - especially tasty barbecued meat and a spicy cabbage dish called *kimchee*.

In 1948, after World War II, the Korean peninsula was officially divided into North Korea and South Korea. North Korea became a **communist** country, but South Korea did not. In 1950 a war broke out between the two. This was the Korean War, which ended in 1953 with the two Koreas remaining separate.

Both North and South Korea have been rebuilt since the war. In 2000 the two countries held talks about joining together again. People were finally allowed to cross between them and meet family members they had not seen since the war, almost 50 years before.

LEARN MORE! READ THESE ARTICLES...
PENINSULA (VOLUME 1) • PYONGYANG, NORTH KOREA (VOLUME 7)
SEOUL, SOUTH KOREA (VOLUME 7)

Pyongyang

Seoul

This monument honours soldiers who fought in the Korean War. The memorial stands near the village of Panmunjom. It lies within a neutral zone established between North and South Korea after the war.
© Robert Holmes/Corbis

North Korea's Age-Old Capital

SEARCH LIGHT

Why have parts of Pyongyang been rebuilt a number of times?

Pyongyang is the capital and largest city of the East Asian country of North Korea. It lies along the Taedong River, close to the Yellow Sea. The name Pyongyang means 'flat land' or 'cosy place' in Korean.

People have lived where Pyongyang now stands for many thousands of years. According to legend, the modern city was started in 1122 BC. Since then it has faced a number of invasions and wars. Armies from China and Japan captured Pyongyang at different times, and much of the city was destroyed in a war between those two countries in the 1890s. The Japanese ruled Pyongyang from 1910 to 1945. In 1948, when Korea was divided into two nations, Pyongyang became the capital of communist North Korea. The city was heavily damaged once again during the Korean War of 1950 to 1953.

Children giving a concert at the Children's Palace in Pyongyang.
© Jeremy Horner/Corbis

A bronze statue of a winged horse towers over Pyongyang. It is meant to remind people of the way the city grew after the end of the Korean War. Other large monuments built in recent years include the wide Arch of Triumph and the Tower of the Juche Idea. (*Juche* means 'self-reliance' - that is, depending on yourself rather than on other people.)

Pyongyang has a university, a medical school, and a school for training Communist Party leaders. There are also a large theatre, a large assembly hall, and a large stadium. In addition, North Korea's main museums and libraries are located in the city.

LEARN MORE! READ THESE ARTICLES...
BERLIN, GERMANY (VOLUME 6) • KOREAN PENINSULA (VOLUME 7)
SEOUL, SOUTH KOREA (VOLUME 7)

DID YOU KNOW?
Wrestling is very popular in North Korea. The largest crowd to watch a live wrestling match was in Pyongyang in 1995, when 190,000 people gathered there to watch The International Sports and Culture Festival for Peace.

The Tower of the Juche Idea rises above the city centre of Pyongyang. The monument celebrates juche ('self-reliance'), a quality favoured by Kim Il-Sung, the first ruler of North Korea.

© Jeremy Horner/Corbis

Answer: Several wars have been fought in Korea over the centuries, and the city has been partially destroyed during the many battles.

21

DID YOU KNOW?
The name Seoul comes from the
Korean word *sorabol*, which means
'capital'.

A Modern Ancient Capital

Seoul, the capital of South Korea, has been attacked and destroyed many times in the past. As a result, it reflects the struggles of Korea in important ways.

In the 16th century Japanese invaders partially destroyed the city. Between 1910 and 1945 Seoul came under Japan's control, and Japan made the city its **colonial** capital. The city was devastated during the Korean War, from 1950 to 1953. Since the 1950s the city has once again been rebuilt. It is sometimes described as an 'endless building site'.

Statues of men in traditional Korean clothing, at the National Folk Museum of South Korea, in Seoul.
© Royalty-Free/Corbis

There is much Chinese influence in Seoul, especially in its design. A long defensive wall with gates, in Chinese style, was built around the city near the end of the 14th century. Parts of the wall and the gates can still be seen.

Today Seoul is a modern city with ancient elements. It has motorways, shopping centres, and tower blocks alongside centuries-old **pagodas**. In the centre of Seoul there are striking palaces and other structures from the city's royal past. Several of these, such as Toksu and Changgyong palaces, are open to the public as museums.

Any tour of Seoul should include a view from Seoul Tower in Namsan Park near the city centre. From the tower you can see many historic and modern sights. These include Kyongbok Palace, one of the royal palaces of the Choson **dynasty**, and Olympic Park, site of the 1988 Summer Olympic Games.

LEARN MORE! READ THESE ARTICLES...
JAPAN: MODERN NATION OF ANCIENT TRADITIONS (VOLUME 7)
A KOREAN FOLKTALE: THE TIGER IN THE TRAP (VOLUME 5)
PYONGYANG, NORTH KOREA (VOLUME 7)

Seoul is home to historic palaces as well as modern high-rise buildings. Changgyong Palace can be seen here in front of the skyline of downtown Seoul.
© Jose Fuste Raga/Corbis

Answer: Seoul has been destroyed and rebuilt several times.

The City of Lady Penh

 Phnom Penh is the capital of the Kingdom of Cambodia in Southeast Asia. It is located at the meeting point of three rivers: the Basak, the Sab, and the Mekong.

Phnom Penh is more than 500 years old. According to legend, a woman named Lady Penh was walking on a hill and found a bronze statue of the Buddha, the founder of the Buddhist religion. There she started the town of Phnom Penh, which means 'Penh Hill'. Her ashes, it is said, were kept in a **pagoda** at the top of the hill.

Phnom Penh was built around the Preah Morokot pagoda. Its floor is paved with tiles of solid silver. The pagoda is built like a tower, with several stories. At the edge of every story, the roof curves upward. It and other stately buildings are near the Royal Palace, where the king and his family live.

Phnom Penh

There are many museums in Phnom Penh. The National Museum has a fine collection of art by the Khmer people, who make up more than 85 percent of the population of Cambodia. The Tuol Sleng Museum is devoted to the memory of the many Cambodians who were killed in the 1970s by Cambodia's communist government. This was a terrible time in the history of the city and country.

The Royal Ballet of Phnom Penh is known the world over. Its ballets are inspired by ancient Buddhist and Hindu legends. There was a time when the dancers performed only for the Cambodian royal family. Now everyone can enjoy them.

LEARN MORE! READ THESE ARTICLES...
ANGKOR WAT (VOLUME 7)
A CAMBODIAN MYTH: MONI MEKHALA AND REAM EYSO (VOLUME 5)
THAILAND (VOLUME 7)

SEARCH LIGHT

What kind of government does Cambodia have? (Hint: Think of the country's full name.)

DID YOU KNOW?

In the 1970s Phnom Penh nearly became a ghost town when Cambodia's rulers forced almost everyone out of the city to work in farm fields.

The Royal Palace in Phnom Penh is home to Cambodia's king and his family.

© Nevada Wier/Corbis

Answer: Cambodia is a kingdom, so in theory it is ruled by a king or a queen. However, in modern times most monarchs have government officials and lawmakers to help run the country.

Cambodia's Treasured Temple

Angkor Wat is a **temple** in the Southeast Asian country of Cambodia. The word *angkor* means 'capital', and *wat* means '**monastery**'. Angkor Wat is more than 800 years old. It is the world's largest religious structure.

The Khmer people are native to Cambodia, and the city of Angkor was once the capital of the Khmer Empire. King Suryavarman II built Angkor Wat. He dedicated the temple to the three Hindu gods Brahma, Vishnu, and Shiva. It was not just a temple but also the government centre of Suryavarman II's empire.

The temple walls are covered with sculptures of Hindu gods. They also show scenes from ancient Khmer history. In addition, there are hundreds of carved statues of *apsara*s, or 'heavenly dancers'. They are seen wearing beautiful costumes, jewellery, and crowns.

About 20 years after the complex was built, a foreign army attacked the Khmers and **looted** the city. King Jayavarman VII, who was ruling the Khmer, felt that the gods had failed him. He became a Buddhist and built a new capital nearby called Angkor Thom. Angkor Wat then became a Buddhist **shrine**. Many of the statues and carvings were replaced by Buddhist art.

After many years, however, the forest grew and covered Angkor Wat. Most people forgot all about it. A French explorer named Henri Mouhot rediscovered the city while travelling on the Mekong River in 1858. In 1992 UNESCO (the United Nations Educational, Scientific and Cultural Organization) named the entire Angkor area a World Heritage site. Today Angkor Wat is one of the main attractions for visitors to Cambodia.

SEARCH LIGHT

Fill in the gaps: Angkor Wat is more than _____ years old and is the world's _____ religious structure.

LEARN MORE! READ THESE ARTICLES...
BUDDHISM (VOLUME 5) • HINDUISM (VOLUME 5)
PHNOM PENH (VOLUME 7)

Tree roots growing on the Ta Prohm temple, part of the temple centre at Angkor, Cambodia.
© Royalty-Free/Corbis

DID YOU KNOW?
When UNESCO named Angkor Wat a World Heritage site, it meant that the place has major importance for the entire world. Being a World Heritage site makes it easier for countries to cooperate to protect a cultural or natural treasure.

Answer: Angkor Wat is more than 800 years old and is the world's largest religious structure.

Indonesians use a process called 'batik' to dye fabrics. The results can be quite colourful.

© Wolfgang Kaehler/Corbis

SEARCH LIGHT

Fill in the gap: Indonesia is a country made up of about 13,670 _____.

Island Nation of Southeast Asia

The Republic of Indonesia is a country of islands lying between the Indian and Pacific oceans. Its capital is Jakarta on the island of Java.

Indonesia is made up of about 13,670 islands, though some are shared with other countries. The largest island is New Guinea, which Indonesia shares with Papua New Guinea. Parts of Borneo, the second largest island in the group, belong to Malaysia and Brunei. Sumatra, Java, and Celebes are the other major islands of Indonesia. Most of Indonesia's people live on these five islands.

Most of the islands are mountainous. Only about one-tenth of the land is used for growing crops, but many of the people make their living from farming. Rice is the main crop grown there. Other crops include coffee, tea, tobacco, and spices. There are also many palm and rubber trees in Indonesia. The country produces many things made of palm oil and is a major supplier of natural rubber.

The **climate** in Indonesia is hot and **humid.** Rain falls heavily throughout the year. Because of that, much of Indonesia is full of rainforests. Mangrove tree swamps are common along the coasts.

Indonesia is known for more than its **natural resources**, though. The people of Indonesia practice special decorative arts throughout the islands. Perhaps the most popular art with tourists is batik, a special way of dyeing fabric. Indonesians are also known for their traditional dance and puppet performances. Puppetry is one of the favourite arts of the islanders themselves.

LEARN MORE! READ THESE ARTICLES...
DANCE (VOLUME 3) • FOLK ARTS AND CRAFTS (VOLUME 3)
VOLCANOES (VOLUME 1)

Jakarta

City of the Gold Pagoda

Yangon is the capital of Myanmar. It is located near the Yangon River. Yangon is the largest city in Myanmar. It is also the country's business centre. In the past the city was known as Rangoon and the country was called Burma.

At one time Yangon and the rest of Myanmar were controlled by Great Britain. The centre of the city, known as the Cantonment, was planned by the British. It is laid out in a grid pattern. Streets run north to south and east to west. As Yangon's population increased, new settlements were built around the Cantonment.

If you visit Yangon, you'll find many interesting places to see. The most famous building there is the Shwe Dagon **Pagoda**. It is a great Buddhist temple on a hill. The pagoda is a solid brick structure that is completely covered with gold. It has been a place of **pilgrimage** for many

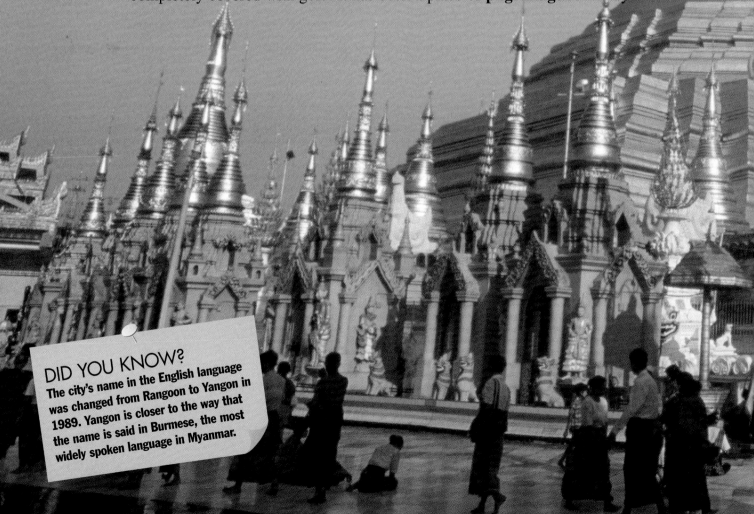

DID YOU KNOW?
The city's name in the English language was changed from Rangoon to Yangon in 1989. Yangon is closer to the way that the name is said in Burmese, the most widely spoken language in Myanmar.

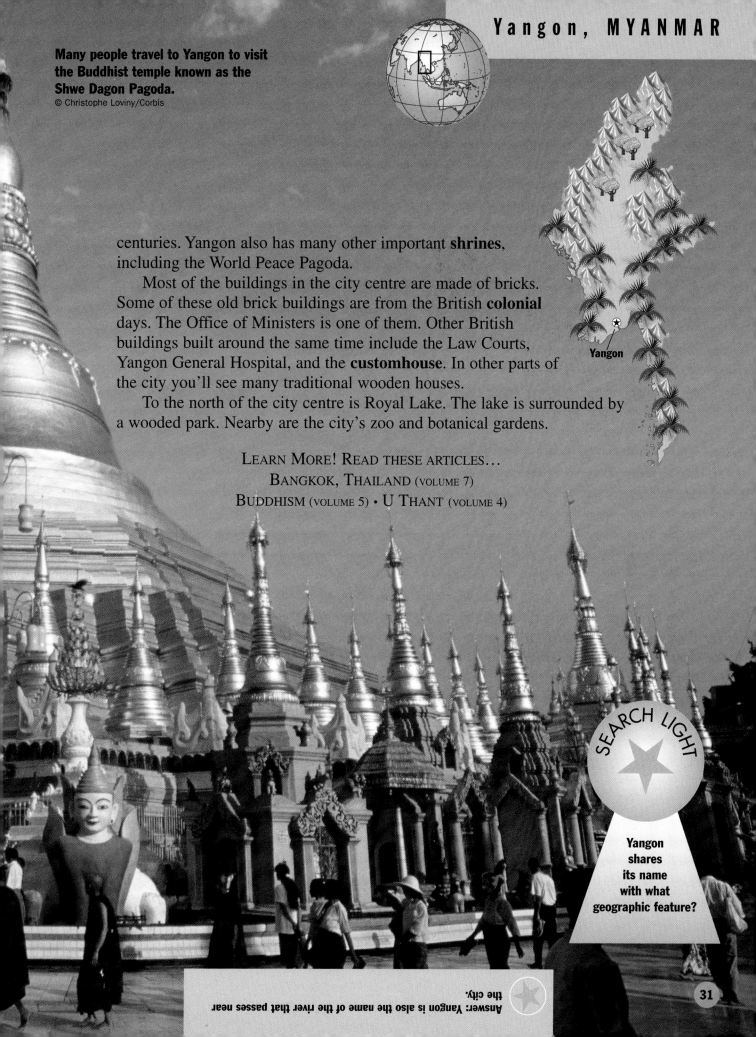

Many people travel to Yangon to visit the Buddhist temple known as the Shwe Dagon Pagoda.
© Christophe Loviny/Corbis

Yangon

centuries. Yangon also has many other important **shrines**, including the World Peace Pagoda.

Most of the buildings in the city centre are made of bricks. Some of these old brick buildings are from the British **colonial** days. The Office of Ministers is one of them. Other British buildings built around the same time include the Law Courts, Yangon General Hospital, and the **customhouse**. In other parts of the city you'll see many traditional wooden houses.

To the north of the city centre is Royal Lake. The lake is surrounded by a wooded park. Nearby are the city's zoo and botanical gardens.

LEARN MORE! READ THESE ARTICLES...
BANGKOK, THAILAND (VOLUME 7)
BUDDHISM (VOLUME 5) • U THANT (VOLUME 4)

SEARCH LIGHT

Yangon shares its name with what geographic feature?

Answer: Yangon is also the name of the river that passes near the city.

SEARCH LIGHT

Find and correct the error in the following sentence: The Philippines are a large group of islands in the Indian Ocean.

DID YOU KNOW?

The most famous Filipino athlete of all time is Rafael ('Paeng') Nepomuceno. He is a professional bowler who is in the International Bowling Hall of Fame in St. Louis, Missouri, in the United States.

Tropical Island Republic

The Republic of the Philippines is made up of about 7,100 islands in the Pacific Ocean along the south-eastern coast of Asia. The two main islands of the Philippines are Luzon, in the north, and Mindanao, in the south. Manila, the capital and most important port, is on Luzon. Most of the larger islands have mountains and dormant, or 'sleeping', volcanoes.

Being an island country and in the tropics, the Philippines has a climate that's warm and **humid**, with a lot of rain. The eastern islands are sometimes soaked by **typhoons**. These strong storms are called 'hurricanes' in other parts of the world.

Watered by all that rain are nearly 10,000 kinds of flowering plant and fern. There are 800 kinds of orchid in the Philippines. Some are very rare. Important trees of the Philippine forests include pine and lauan, which is better known as Philippine mahogany. The country's animals include monkeys, water buffalo, and more than 50 kinds of bat. The monkey-eating eagle is one of the rarer birds.

Farming is an important business in the Philippines. The people grow mostly rice and maize. They also grow sugarcane, bananas, and pineapples. The Philippines also produces many coconuts. Most of the farming is done on the central plain of Luzon.

The Philippine people are known as Filipinos. They speak many languages. The official languages are Pilipino and English. The English language came to the Philippines when the country was led by the United States after the Spanish-American War of 1898.

LEARN MORE! READ THESE ARTICLES…
BATS (VOLUME 12) • INDONESIA (VOLUME 7)
VOLCANOES (VOLUME 1)

Manila

A woman sells colourful flowers at a market in Manila, the capital of the Philippines.
© David Samuel Robbins/Corbis

Answer: The Philippines are a large group of islands in the Pacific Ocean.

33

SEARCH LIGHT

Singapore has four official languages - Malay, Mandarin Chinese, Tamil (an Indian language), and English. Most countries have one or two. Why do you think Singapore has so many?

The Lion City

The Republic of Singapore is a small island nation in Southeast Asia. Singapore is also the name of the country's main island and of its capital city. Legend says that a prince named the island Singapura, meaning 'lion city', because he thought he saw a lion there.

Singapore Island and about 60 little nearby islands make up the country. All these islands lie off the southern tip of the Malay **Peninsula**. Singapore Island is shaped like a diamond. It is linked to the country of Malaysia on the Malay Peninsula by a road and railway that cross the water of the Johor **Strait**.

Singapore

As of 1995, almost 3 million people lived in this small island nation. That makes Singapore one of the most crowded countries in the world. But Singapore is also one of the most well-to-do Asian nations because it has been a busy world shipping port for a long time. People have moved there from all parts of Asia, giving Singapore a rich and varied cultural **heritage**. Most people speak the Malay language, but Mandarin Chinese, Tamil (an Indian language), and English are also official languages.

Singapore's weather is hot and very rainy - a typical **monsoon** climate. The lowlands often flood when it rains hard, but the rainy weather is good for plants. While only a few of Singapore's native plants remain, patches of original rainforests still survive. There are some original **mangrove** forests on the main island's north-western side. And people often call Singapore city the 'Garden City' because of its many parks, gardens, and tree-lined streets.

> ## DID YOU KNOW?
> If you want to give a gift to someone from Singapore, you shouldn't give a clock or a handkerchief. These objects are linked with death or funerals. Umbrellas are not good gifts either - they are associated with accidents.

LEARN MORE! READ THESE ARTICLES...
INDONESIA (VOLUME 7) • ISLANDS (VOLUME 1)
RAINFORESTS (VOLUME 1)

Singapore is sometimes known as the 'Lion City'. Its symbol is a merlion, a creature that is half lion and half fish.
© Earl & Nazima Kowall/Corbis

Answer: Singapore's four official languages reflect the fact that people from many different cultures have moved there. Also, being a busy and successful world port means that people from all over the world live, work, and pass through Singapore.

DID YOU KNOW?
Long ago, the kings of Thailand gave white elephants to people who upset them. No one could refuse such a rare gift, but owners often went bankrupt because caring for the elephants was very expensive. Today the phrase 'white elephant' is used to describe a gift that nobody wants.

Kingdom of Southeast Asia

The people of the Kingdom of Thailand often describe their land as looking like an elephant's head. The trunk is the south. The ear is the northeast. The top of the head is the mountainous north. The mouth is the **delta** and harbour of the Chao Phraya River, where you will also find Bangkok, the country's capital and chief port. The plains of the river's **basin** make up the elephant's eyes.

Monsoons shape the weather in most of Thailand. They bring lots of rain from May to September. The heavy rain was good for the forests that once covered half of the country. But since 1970 many of the forests have been cut down by loggers. Forests have also been cleared to provide land for farming, especially for growing rice, the main food crop. The remaining forests in Thailand contain teak, bamboo, palms, and rattan. All of these are used to make things to sell.

The royal palace plays an important part in preserving traditional Thai culture. Many ceremonies are held at the palace. One of these is the yearly *kathina* ('cloth') ceremony, in which people present gifts to Buddhist **monks** who have just returned from a period of **seclusion**.

Thai cooking has become very popular in many countries outside Thailand. Seafood, meats, and vegetables are often flavoured with coconut milk and peanuts in spicy and delicious curries, or stews, and served over rice or noodles. If there is a Thai restaurant in your area, you can enjoy a sample of Thailand's famous **cuisine**.

Bangkok

LEARN MORE! READ THESE ARTICLES...
ELEPHANTS (VOLUME 12) • MONASTICISM (VOLUME 5)
VIETNAM (VOLUME 7)

SEARCH LIGHT

Look at the map of Thailand. Do you think it looks like an elephant? Can you make out the head, ear, and trunk?

Here, Buddhist monks in Thailand take part in a special ceremony. Buddhism, the national religion, plays an important role in Thai culture.
© Jeremy Horner/Corbis

Answer: There's no one answer. Compare your answer with your friends' answers.

City of Angels

Bangkok is the capital of Thailand and the country's largest and most important port. The Thai people call the city Krung Thep, which means 'city of angels'. Bangkok spreads across both sides of the Chao Phraya River. From the river a network of **canals** spreads through the city.

Goods sold from small boats in a floating market in Bangkok.
© Louis K. Meisel Gallery/Corbis

The Grand Palace, where the kings of Thailand once lived, stands on the river's east bank. The palace is surrounded by walls. Also within these walls is Wat Phra Kaeo, a temple full of Thai art treasures. It holds the Emerald Buddha, the holiest statue of the Buddha in all of Thailand.

There are many other Buddhist temples, or *wat*s, along the banks of the Chao Phraya River. A *wat* usually has living quarters for monks, **shrines** for **meditation**, towers, and a meeting place. Some of the *wat*s are decorated with beautiful carvings. The Temple of Dawn, or Wat Arun, is one of these.

Wat Pho is the oldest and largest *wat* in Bangkok. It has the largest reclining Buddha and the largest collection of Buddha images in Thailand. People call Wat Pho the first university in Thailand. An early king had **texts** carved in stone and set around the temple so that people could read and learn from them.

In Bangkok's famous floating markets, merchants sell fruits, vegetables, flowers, and other items from boats in the canals. Shoppers step from boat to boat as they look at all the things to buy.

LEARN MORE! READ THESE ARTICLES...
BUDDHISM (VOLUME 5) · SCULPTURE (VOLUME 3)
THAILAND (VOLUME 7)

SEARCH LIGHT

The name Krung Thep means
a) 'grand palace.'
b) 'city of angels.'
c) 'emerald Buddha.'

These Buddhist monks walk on the grounds of one of Bangkok's famous temples, the Wat Phra Kaeo. Inside the temple is a sacred image called the Emerald Buddha. Buddhism is the city's main religion.
© Paul Almasy/Corbis

North and South

The Socialist Republic of Vietnam is located in Southeast Asia, near China, Laos, and Cambodia. It is made up of what for many years were two countries: North Vietnam (the Democratic Republic of Vietnam) and South Vietnam (the Republic of Vietnam). After a long war, the two countries were reunited in 1976. The capital of Vietnam is Hanoi.

Most people know of Vietnam because of its wars. The one that led to the reunification of North and South Vietnam began in the 1950s. The **communists** who ruled North Vietnam wanted to bring the two countries together under their leadership. South Vietnam, with support from the United States, tried to stop them. During the late 1960s and the early 1970s, both the Vietnamese and the Americans suffered great losses. Many people were killed, and Vietnamese cities and much of the countryside were badly damaged. South Vietnam surrendered to North Vietnam in 1975.

In spite of the troubles Vietnam has faced, it still has a number of interesting places to visit. Hanoi has centuries-old temples as well as modern art and history museums. Bustling Ho Chi Minh City (formerly Saigon, capital of South Vietnam) has Buddhist **pagodas** and a **cathedral** among its attractions.

Most of Vietnam's people are farmers. Much of the farmland is used for growing rice. There are also farms that grow coffee, tea, rubber, sugarcane, soybeans, and coconuts. The people often eat meals of rice with fish.

Hanoi

SEARCH LIGHT

Fill in the gaps: Present-day Vietnam is the result of joining _____ and _____ Vietnam in the 1970s.

LEARN MORE! READ THESE ARTICLES...
BUDDHISM (VOLUME 5) • HANOI, VIETNAM (VOLUME 7)
RICE (VOLUME 10)

DID YOU KNOW?

French is one of the languages spoken in Vietnam, and French cooking is part of Vietnam's cuisine. Sound odd? France once ruled the country as a colony, until the Vietnamese gained their independence in the 1950s.

Farmers work in a rice paddy in central Vietnam.

Answer: Present-day Vietnam is the result of joining North and South Vietnam in the 1970s.

Capital of Reunited Vietnam

SEARCH LIGHT

Hanoi has been the capital of Vietnam since 1976. It is located on the western bank of the Red River. *Ha* means 'river' and *noi* means 'within'. Hanoi has been called by many other names in the past. First it was Dong Kinh, then Tonquin, Tonkin, and finally Hanoi.

From the 1880s to the 1940s, Hanoi was the centre of French-controlled Southeast Asia. Then Hanoi became the capital of North Vietnam when it went to war with South Vietnam. The North defeated the South in 1975. The two parts of the country became one again, and Hanoi became the capital.

The streets in Hanoi are named for the things that used to be sold there long ago. Pho Hang Bun was where noodles were sold. Pho Hang Ma was the place for paper products. And Pho Hang Bac was the road for buying jewellery. Some streets have **shrines** dedicated to the gods of these trades.

During the Vietnam War, many of Hanoi's monuments and palaces were destroyed. One that survived was Lake Hoan Kiem. It was once part of the Red River and was called Luc Thuy, or 'Green Water', because of its colour. Two interesting historical places are the Co Loa **citadel** and the Temple of Literature. The citadel is what remains of an ancient capital. The thousand-year-old temple is a shrine dedicated to Confucius, the great Chinese thinker. The Temple of the Trung Sisters is an interesting place to visit too. It honours two women who led a rebellion against the Chinese Han dynasty in the 1st century AD.

If Pho Hang Bun means 'street of noodles' and Pho Hang Bac means 'street of jewellery', what do you think Pho Hang means?

DID YOU KNOW?

Dong Kinh, the original name of Hanoi, became Tonquin only because Europeans had trouble pronouncing the name.

LEARN MORE! READ THESE ARTICLES...
CONFUCIUS (VOLUME 5)
PHNOM PENH, CAMBODIA (VOLUME 7) • VIETNAM (VOLUME 7)

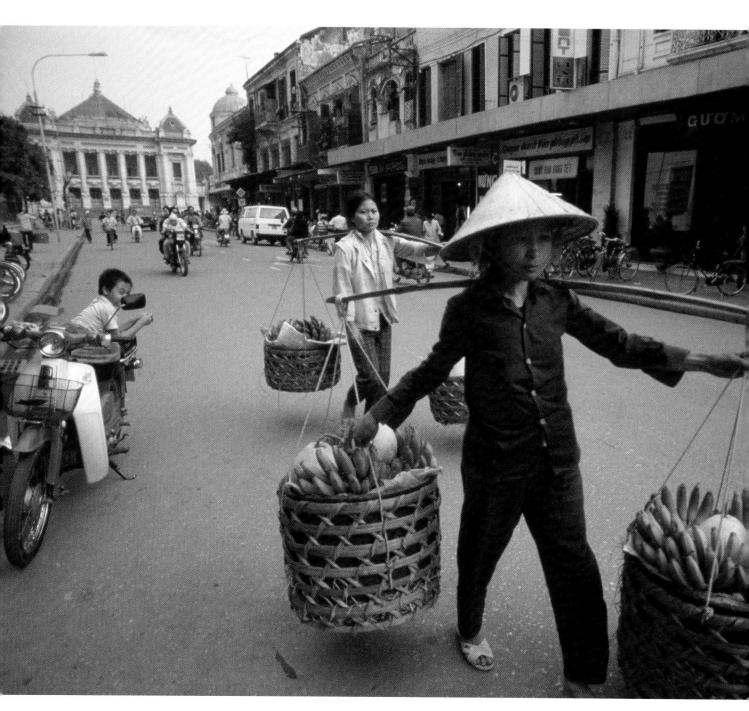

In this picture you can see many sides of Hanoi. Women
sell produce from nearby farms, modern motorcycles and
cars share space with bicycles, and in the background is
a French-built opera house from colonial times.
© Steve Raymer/Corbis

Answer: If you guessed that Pho Hang means 'street of,' then
you're right. It can also mean 'district.'

43

SEARCH LIGHT

Unscramble these words connected with Afghanistan:
- blaKu
- niHud shuK
- tinamouns

DID YOU KNOW?

Conflict is not new to Afghanistan. During the 1800s, Russia and England supported different tribal groups in Afghanistan. This led to many battles and wars in the region. The Europeans called this contest the 'Great Game'.

Mountain Country

Afghanistan is a dry country in southern Central Asia. Kabul is Afghanistan's capital city. Mountains cover a large part of the country. The Pamir Mountains rise in the north-east, and the giant Hindu Kush range spreads across the country from north-east to south-west. Many of Afghanistan's rivers get their water from the melting snow and **glaciers** in the mountains. The Kabul River provides water for the fertile valleys and **basins** around the cities of Kabul and Jalalabad.

Not much of Afghanistan's land can be used for farming, though. It is either too rocky or too dry. Only farmers who live in the river valleys where water is available are able to grow crops. They mostly grow wheat, maize, grapes, and rice. Instead of farming, many people raise herds of sheep, goats, cattle, or camels.

For centuries Afghanistan was ruled by a king. It suffered a long civil war in the 1980s when the Soviet Union supported Afghanistan's **communist** government. In the 1990s a Muslim group overthrew the government and then fought amongst themselves. Finally one group, called the Taliban, took control. They made many strict laws and took away a lot of the Afghan people's rights. Many people around the world were upset by this.

In 2001 the United States was attacked by terrorists. The U.S. government blamed the terrorism on al-Qaeda, a Muslim group supported by the Taliban. A few weeks later the United States, Britain, and other allies attacked Afghanistan and forced the Taliban from power. The new government restored many of the rights of the Afghan people that the Taliban had taken away.

Kabul

LEARN MORE! READ THESE ARTICLES...
ISLAM (VOLUME 5) • MOUNTAINS (VOLUME 1)
PAKISTAN (VOLUME 7)

Complex designs cover a wall of a mosque in the city of Mazar-e Sharif, Afghanistan. Many Muslims believe that inside the mosque is the tomb of Ali, the son-in-law of Muhammad, the founder of the Islamic religion.
© Charles & Josette Lenars/Corbis

Answer: - blaku = Kabul
- nihud shuk = Hindu Kush
- tinamous = mountains

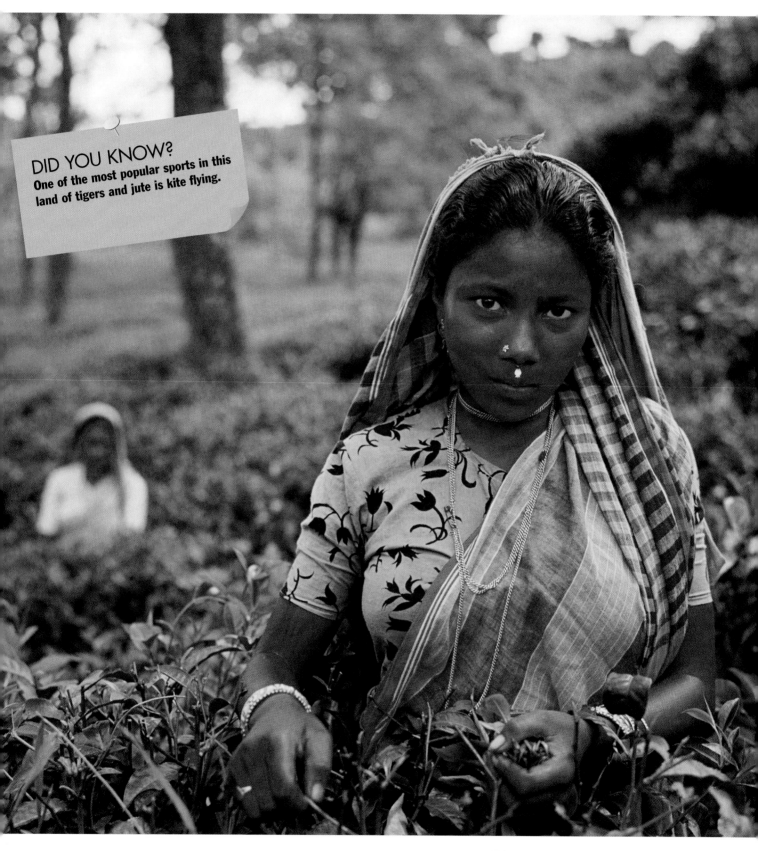

This young woman is picking tea leaves in a field in Bangladesh. Tea is one of the country's major crops.

© Roger Wood/Corbis

Land of the Bengals

Bangladesh is a small densely populated country in South Asia. It's also a young country, born only in 1971. Before that it was called East Pakistan. But the area it lies in is traditionally known as Bengal.

East Pakistan was part of the country of Pakistan. The people of East Pakistan wanted their freedom, and they won it after fighting a war with the help of the neighbouring country of India. Today Bangladesh shares a language (Bengali) and culture with the Indian state of West Bengal. Most of the people are of the Islamic faith, though a number are Hindu.

Bangladesh is generally hot and **humid**. Two major rivers - the Ganges (Ganga) and the Brahmaputra - come together there as the Padma River. Summer brings heavy rains. Every two or three years the Brahmaputra River floods the countryside, killing many people and damaging crops and houses.

Bangladesh's capital, Dhaka, is divided into Old and New Dhaka. In Old Dhaka you can see many styles of buildings, most notably Mughal (Islamic) monuments, gardens, and mosques. In the maze of crowded narrow lanes, bazaars sell everything from bracelets to silk to books.

Dhaka

In the **fertile** central region of Bangladesh, many crops are grown. These include rice and jute, a fibre often used to make sacks and mats. Jute is sold to other countries. Parts of Bangladesh are covered with forests - bamboo trees in the east and mangrove swamps along the coast. Elephants, bears, deer, and monkeys live in the forests and grasslands. But the country's best-known animal is the Bengal tiger - larger than all the big cats except the Siberian tiger.

LEARN MORE! READ THESE ARTICLES...
BAMBOO (VOLUME 10) • PAKISTAN (VOLUME 7)
TIGERS (VOLUME 12)

SEARCH LIGHT

Fill in
the gap:
Thimphu sits
high above sea level
in a valley of the
_____ Mountains.

Schoolchildren sit on a hill above Thimphu. Before the
1960s the city had no formal schools except ones that
taught religion. But since then great progress has been
made in non-religious education.
© Karan Kapoor/Corbis

City in the Heart of the Himalayas

Thimphu is the capital of Bhutan, a small country in South Asia. It is a small city located in a valley in the heart of the Himalaya Mountains.

The people of Thimphu are not allowed to build houses in just any way they choose. There are strict rules for how all buildings must look. Buildings must be a certain height, and they have to follow the traditional building style of Bhutan. The similar-looking buildings give Thimphu a special look.

The Tashi Chho *dzong* is a good example of the Bhutanese style of building. It is styled like a fortress, but it was originally a **monastery**. It's been remodelled and now also houses the offices of the royal government.

Farming is very important to the people of Thimphu. All **fertile** soil is used for growing crops - even the land around the royal palace. The main crops are rice, maize, and wheat.

Tourists usually like to visit the vegetable market in Thimphu. At one end of the market, you'll find people selling **handicrafts** and other locally made items. These include Buddhist prayer wheels and flags, baskets, hand-woven and hand-knitted clothes, and many different kinds of hats. Another interesting place is the memorial *chorten*, or small **shrine**, at the temple called Changangkha Lhakhang. And you should make time to go up the hill known as Sangay Gang. From there you'll get a spectacular view of Thimphu.

DID YOU KNOW?
The government of Bhutan limits the number of tourists who can enter the country. One result is that Thimphu is a quiet city with little of the crowding common in other capitals.

LEARN MORE! READ THESE ARTICLES...
KATHMANDU, NEPAL (VOLUME 7)
MONASTICISM (VOLUME 5)
MOUNTAINS (VOLUME 1)

Answer: Thimphu sits high above sea level in a valley of the Himalaya Mountains.

49

DID YOU KNOW?
In India's capital, New Delhi, is a slender five-storey-tall tower built by early Muslim kings. It's in a group of buildings called the Qutub Minar. The Muslim conquerors made the buildings and tower from pieces of Hindu and Jain temples.

SEARCH LIGHT

True or false? A *chaitya* is a place where Hindus pray.

Land of Temples and Shrines

India is a country of more than a billion people. The people speak dozens of languages, including Hindi, Bengali, Telugu, and Tamil. Many also speak English. The country is the birthplace of two major religions: Hinduism and Buddhism. Both were founded in ancient times, but many people in India still practice them, especially Hinduism. Other religions in India include Islam, Christianity, and Sikhism. The country's capital is New Delhi.

People from all over the world travel to India to see its many beautiful and historic buildings. Long ago, for instance, Buddhists built dome-shaped **shrines** called *stupa*s. These were built in places where the founder of the religion, the Buddha, lived, visited, or preached. Some of the most famous *stupa*s are at Sanchi and Sarnath. A *chaitya* is a Buddhist temple, or place where people pray together. There are some beautiful *chaitya*s among a group of caves carved out of cliffs at Ajanta. The Ajanta caves are also known for their paintings. Though the paintings are about 2,000 years old, they still look bright and beautiful.

India also has several Hindu rock temples. The Kailash Temple at Ellora is carved out of solid rock. So are the sculptured temples of Khajuraho. The stone *ratha*s, or shrines, in Mahabalipuram are also remarkable.

Many tourists like to see India's grand **mausoleums**, where important people are buried. The Taj Mahal, one of the most beautiful sites in the world, is the mausoleum complex Emperor Shah Jahan built for his queen in the 1600s.

New Delhi

LEARN MORE! READ THESE ARTICLES...
MAHATMA GANDHI (VOLUME 4)
A SOUTH ASIAN TALE: THE MONKEY AND
THE STRING OF PEARLS (VOLUME 5)
TAJ MAHAL (VOLUME 7)

The Buddhist religion began in India many years ago. These caves in western India were used as temples and monasteries by early followers of the religion. The walls of the caves are covered with religious paintings.

Answer: FALSE. A *chaitya* is a place where Buddhists pray.

Wonder of the World

SEARCH LIGHT

Find and correct the mistake in the following sentence: The Taj Mahal was built as a palace for Shah Jahan's wife.

Several hundred years ago most of India was conquered and ruled by the Mughals, who followed the religion of Islam. When the emperor Jahangir ruled over northern India, his son, Prince Khurram, married Arjumand Banu Baygam. Prince Khurram called his wife Mumtaz Mahal, meaning 'chosen one of the palace'. The two were almost always together, and together they had 14 children.

Prince Khurram became emperor in 1628 and was called Emperor Shah Jahan. But three years later, Mumtaz Mahal died while having a baby. Shah Jahan was heartbroken. He decided to build the most beautiful monument to his wife. He had the best **architects** design it in a perfect blend of Indian, Persian, and Islamic styles. Beginning in about 1632, over 20,000 workers laboured for 22 years to create what was to become one of the wonders of the world.

The great monument was called the Taj Mahal (a form of Mumtaz Mahal's name). It was built in the city of Agra, India, the capital of Shah Jahan's empire. Its several buildings sit in a large garden on the south bank of the Yamuna River. From the garden's south gateway you can see the front of the white marble **mausoleum**. It contains the tombs of Mumtaz Mahal and Shah Jahan. The mausoleum stands on a high marble platform surrounded by four minarets, or towers. Many of its walls and pillars shimmer with **inlaid** gemstones, including lapis lazuli, jade, crystal, turquoise, and amethyst. And verses from the Koran (the Muslim holy book) appear on many parts of the Taj.

Many visitors still come to the Taj Mahal. To help protect and care for it for many years to come, the Taj was made a World Heritage site in 1983.

LEARN MORE! READ THESE ARTICLES...
ARCHITECTURE (VOLUME 3) • INDIA (VOLUME 7)
KORAN (VOLUME 5)

DID YOU KNOW?
According to tradition, Shah Jahan planned to have a tomb built for himself across the river from the Taj Mahal, with a bridge connecting the two. But he was removed from power and imprisoned by his son before his plan could be carried out.

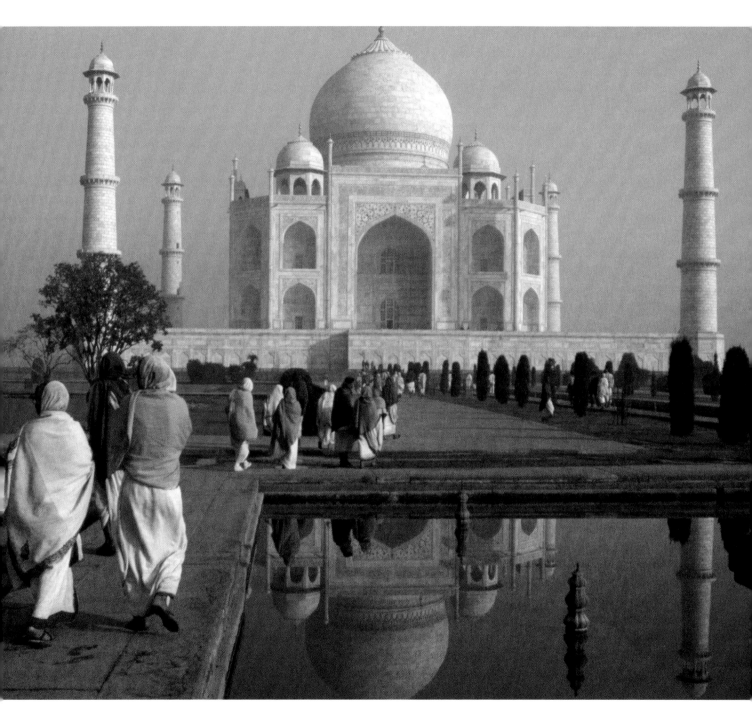

Visitors flock to see the breathtaking Taj Mahal in Agra, India. Many people in the city claim to be descendants of the 20,000 workers who built the structure.
© Vince Streano/Corbis

Answer: The Taj Mahal was built as a tomb for Shah Jahan's wife.

This village in Nepal sits on many terraces, or steps, cut into the side of a mountain. Most of the country's farms are terraced. Each terrace helps the land soak up water that might otherwise simply slide downhill.

Country of Mount Everest

Nepal is a mountainous country between India and the Tibet **Autonomous** Region of China. Its capital is Kathmandu. Mount Everest, the world's tallest mountain, stands on the border between China and Nepal. The people of Nepal call it Sagarmatha. Everest and many other of the world's highest peaks belong to the mountain range called the Himalayas.

Rain falls in Nepal between June and September, which is good for farming. Among the crops grown are rice, sugarcane, and wheat. Most of the fields are in steps, or terraces. Farmers also raise sheep, cattle, and the longhaired oxen known as 'yaks'.

Nepal has many forests in the valleys and lower mountains. The country's wild animals include sheep, goats, and deer. The snow leopard and the great Indian rhinoceros are also present but are seldom seen.

The Himalayas are famous for the Yeti, or **Abominable** Snowman. Some people point to strange footprints in the snow and say that only a monstrous Yeti could have made them. But most scientists say that the footprints are actually made by bears and that the Yeti is only a legend.

Even if you don't see an Abominable Snowman, there are still many interesting sights in Nepal. Lumbini is said to have been the birthplace of the Buddha, a religious leader whose followers are called Buddhists. The valley of Kathmandu also has nearly 2,500 ancient temples and other places of worship. Followers of the religion of Hinduism think that the temple of Lord Pashupatinath, a guardian spirit, is the holiest place in Nepal.

Kathmandu

LEARN MORE! READ THESE ARTICLES…
BUDDHA (VOLUME 5) • HINDUISM (VOLUME 5)
KATHMANDU, NEPAL (VOLUME 7)

SEARCH LIGHT

Does the Yeti exist?

Answer: There has been no proof that the Yeti exists - no photos, films, or living examples. On the other hand, most animals that are 'discovered' by scientists are known for a long time by the local people. Some local people claim to have seen a Yeti.

City of Palaces

Kathmandu is the capital city of the mountainous South Asian country of Nepal. Kathmandu means 'wooden temple'. The city got its present name more than 400 years ago, when a temple was built there from the wood of a single tree. The temple still stands in Kathmandu's central square. It is one of many temples in the city built by followers of the Buddhist and Hindu religions.

Even older than the temple is the palace of the Malla family. The palace was built by a raja. Raja is a title given to many princes and rulers in South Asia. The main gate of the palace is guarded by a figure of the monkey god Hanuman. The palace has a small adjoining square where there are many **pagoda**-style temples.

Many other palaces stand just outside Kathmandu. The grandest among these is the Singha Palace. It used to be the residence of the prime ministers of Nepal. The palace is now the government **secretariat**.

The city also has a large parade ground. In the centre of the ground is a stone platform surrounding a tree. This place was used long ago for making important announcements to the army.

It is interesting to visit Kathmandu during festival time. And there are many festivals. In spring there is the Machendra Jatra, when the image of the god Machendra is carried in a long **procession** through the streets. In late summer is the Gai Jatra, a festival of cows. As part of the autumn festival called Indra Jatra, a young girl is dressed up as the goddess Devi and carried through the city.

SEARCH LIGHT

Fill in the gaps: Kathmandu means '_____ _____' because a temple was built there from a single _____.

LEARN MORE! READ THESE ARTICLES...
BUDDHISM (VOLUME 5) • HINDUISM (VOLUME 5) • NEPAL (VOLUME 7)

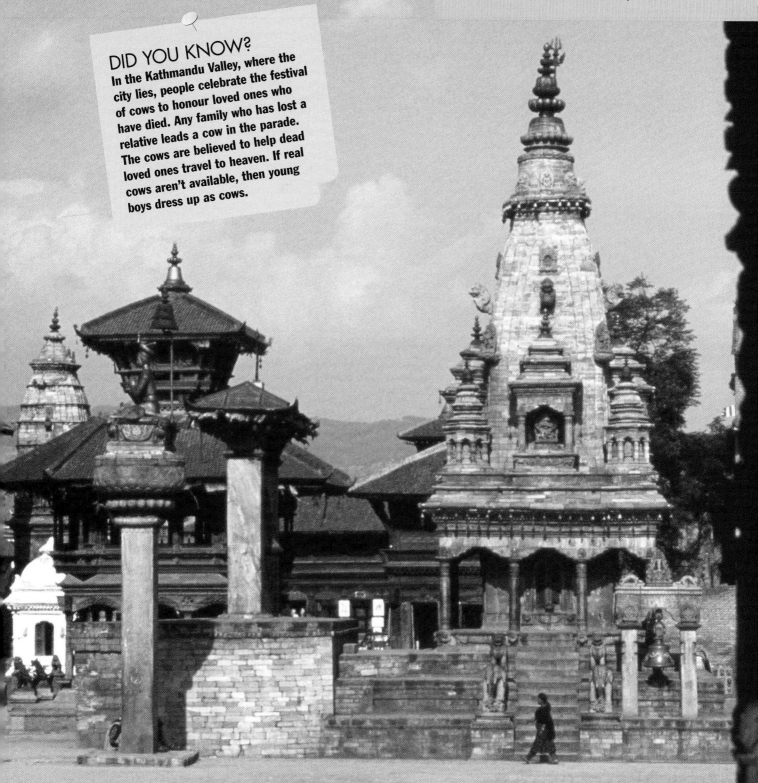

Many of Kathmandu's temples and monuments are clustered in Durbar Square, at the centre of the city's historic district.
© Macduff Everton/Corbis

Answer: Kathmandu means 'wooden temple' because a temple was built there from a single tree.

SEARCH LIGHT

True or false? Pakistan used to be part of India.

A group sets up camp in the Karakoram Range in Pakistan.
© Galen Rowell/Corbis

58

A Young Country with an Ancient History

Pakistan is a country in South Asia. India is its largest neighbour. For many years Pakistan and India were a single country known as British India. Pakistan was created to provide a separate homeland for India's Muslims. It became an independent country in 1947. Its capital is Islamabad.

Islamabad

Pakistan was established in two sections, East Pakistan and West Pakistan. Later, in 1971, East Pakistan became a separate country called Bangladesh.

Although Pakistan is a young country, it has a rich history. It was the site of the ancient Indus civilization. This was one of the largest of the early city-based civilizations. Pakistan is also home to many historic **mosques**, tombs, and **shrines**. Some of these are hundreds of years old.

Pakistan is a rugged place. In the north are the mountains of the Karakoram Range and the Himalayas. Some of the world's tallest mountains are part of these ranges. Huge **glaciers** and roaring rivers cross this landscape. Other parts of the country are very dry. Pakistan's natural plant life is mainly grass and bushes. But on the slopes of the Himalayas, oak, cherry, cedar, and pine trees grow. Brown bears, black Himalayan bears, leopards, and wild sheep are found in the northern mountains. The rare snow leopard is found there also.

Most of Pakistan's people speak Urdu. But Punjabi, Sindhi, Pashto, and Balochi are also spoken. Many people can also speak English.

Many Pakistanis are farmers. They grow rice and cotton. Some people make a living from forestry and fishing. Others make beautiful carpets and do fine **embroidery**.

LEARN MORE! READ THESE ARTICLES…
BANGLADESH (VOLUME 7)
MOHAMMED ALI JINNAH (VOLUME 4)
PAKISTAN: LAND OF THE INDUS CIVILIZATION (VOLUME 7)

DID YOU KNOW?

The official emblem, or symbol, of Pakistan features the crescent-and-star symbol of the national religion, Islam. The emblem also displays what were originally Pakistan's four main crops: cotton, tea, wheat, and jute.

Answer: TRUE.

Land of the Indus Civilization

There are some great mysteries in history. One of the greatest concerns the ancient Indus civilization. Nearly 4,000 years ago, the Indus people and their civilization disappeared. Why did this happen? If there's an answer to be found, it lies in what is now the country of Pakistan.

Ancient stone tablets containing an early form of writing.
© Charles & Josette Lenars/Corbis

For thousands of years, no trace remained of the Indus civilization. Then, beginning in 1921, its remains were discovered by **archaeologists**. Buried near the Indus River in Sindh, now in Pakistan, were bricks, seals (imprinting stamps), water **ducts**, and fossils. They told an interesting story.

The remains showed that the Indus people had lived in two large cities and more than 100 towns and villages. The two cities were Mohenjo-daro and Harappa. Both had a huge fortress on a raised mound, and houses laid out below.

The Indus people were farmers. They grew wheat, peas, sesame, and cotton. They kept different kinds of cattle and fowl. They may have also kept pigs, camels, and elephants. And they traded. They bought precious metals such as gold, silver, and copper from southern India or perhaps Afghanistan. And they had their own form of writing, with 250 to 500 symbols or letters.

How did the civilization come to an end? Mohenjo-daro was destroyed by outside invaders. But most of the towns were close to the Indus River and were often flooded. It is possible that the region suffered many natural disasters. It also may be that no single thing caused the civilization to decline. No one knows for sure.

LEARN MORE! READ THESE ARTICLES...
FERTILE CRESCENT (VOLUME 7) • FOSSILS (VOLUME 1)
PAKISTAN: A YOUNG COUNTRY WITH AN
ANCIENT HISTORY (VOLUME 7)

DID YOU KNOW?

Although such major cities of the Indus civilization as Mohenjo-daro existed many thousands of years ago, they had very good drainage and sanitation systems. Many houses had their own bathrooms.

Thousands of years ago the Indus River civilization developed in what is now Pakistan. Remains of the civilization's largest city, Mohenjo-daro, can be seen here.
© Paul Almasy/Corbis

SEARCH LIGHT

The people of the Indus Valley civilization disappeared
a) 4,000 years ago.
b) 40,000 years ago.
c) 400 years ago.
d) yesterday.

Answer: a) 4,000 years ago.

Island Nation of Natural Riches

The cloth of your shirt or the lead in your pencil may be from Sri Lanka! Tea is another famous **export** of this island nation.

Sri Lanka lies just south of India in the Indian Ocean. For hundreds of years, it was called Ceylon. In 1972 its name was changed to Sri Lanka. Colombo is Sri Lanka's capital, but the country's **legislature** and law courts are based in the city of Sri Jayewardenepura Kotte.

Most Sri Lankans are farmers. Because the country has a tropical **climate**, with high **humidity** and plenty of rainfall, it is easy to grow rice, tea, sugarcane, rubber trees, and coconut palms. Sri Lankans mine precious gems such as sapphires and rubies. They also produce graphite, the material used to make pencil leads and other products.

Sri Lanka was ruled by different countries for hundreds of years. The Portuguese were the first Europeans to conquer the island. They arrived in 1505. Then the Dutch gained control by promising to help drive the Portuguese away. Finally, in 1802 the British took over the island. They ruled for almost 150 years. Each of these countries wanted to **colonize** the island so they could make money trading its natural goods.

Despite long years of foreign rule, the Sri Lankan people have preserved their traditional sculpture, painting, and **architecture**. The ancient religions of Buddhism and Hinduism have strongly influenced the arts in Sri Lanka. The country's many Buddhist and Hindu temples, with their dramatic ceremonies, are a focus of the island's cultural life.

Colombo

LEARN MORE! READ THESE ARTICLES...
BUDDHISM (VOLUME 5)
HINDUISM (VOLUME 5) • INDIA (VOLUME 7)

SEARCH LIGHT

Which of these products does Sri Lanka sell to other countries?
a) tea, tobacco, and coconuts
b) tea, coconuts, and gold
c) tea, rubber, and gems

People in Sri Lanka practice a
traditional form of fishing using stilts.
© Torleif Svensson/Corbis

DID YOU KNOW?
In Sri Lanka some people believe it's
bad luck to have a chameleon (a kind
of lizard) cross your path.

Answer: c) tea, rubber, and gems

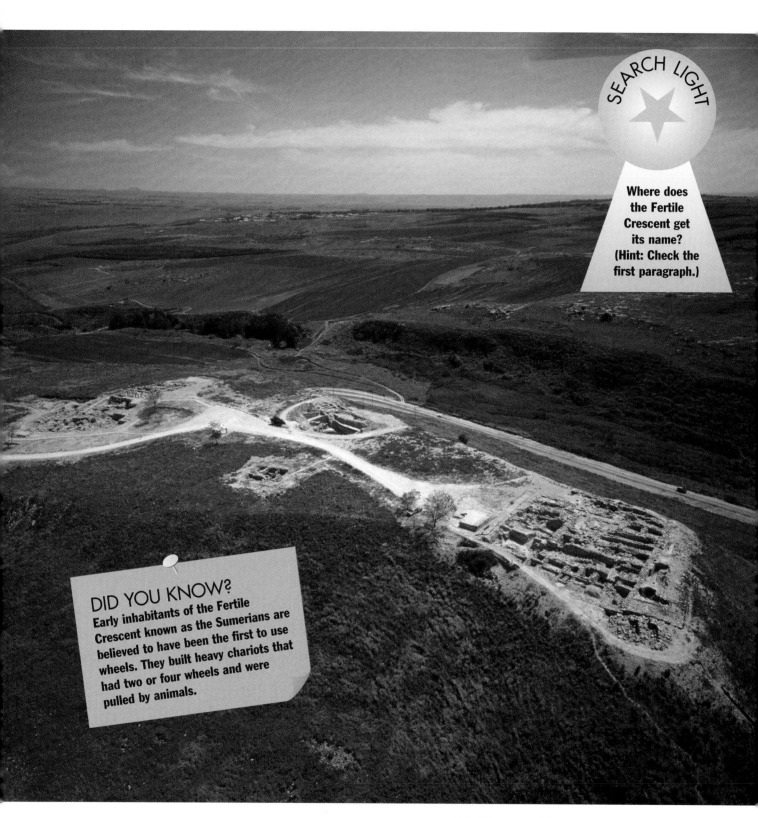

DID YOU KNOW?
Early inhabitants of the Fertile Crescent known as the Sumerians are believed to have been the first to use wheels. They built heavy chariots that had two or four wheels and were pulled by animals.

Scientists uncovered these ruins (seen from an airplane) of the ancient city of Hazor, in what is now northern Israel. Located on an important trade route through the Fertile Crescent, the city blossomed during biblical times.

© Richard T. Nowitz/Corbis

Cradle of Civilization

The Fertile Crescent is an area in the Middle East. It is called that for two reasons. First, the land was fertile - that is, rich and productive - for growing crops and could feed many people. Many of the earliest civilizations started here. And, second, the area formed the shape of a crescent, which is what the Moon looks like when most of it is in shadow.

The Fertile Crescent is located between the Arabian Desert and the mountains of Armenia. The Tigris and Euphrates rivers are major

Ancient sculpture from the Fertile Crescent showing merchants carrying goods on horseback.
© Archivo Iconografico, S.A./Corbis

waterways within the Fertile Crescent. Some people also include the Nile River valley of Egypt as part of the region. The other modern countries that lie in the area of the Fertile Crescent include Jordan, Syria, Lebanon, Israel, Iraq, and part of Turkey.

This area was particularly good for farming long ago, especially in the Nile valley. That is why it is called 'fertile'. It is still a farming area today. Just as in the past, people today use man-made methods of watering crops. This is called 'irrigation'. In fact, it would be impossible to grow anything without irrigation in some places there.

For many years historians believed that the earliest civilization started in the Fertile Crescent. Much later, when scientists discovered new methods for finding out how old a place or a thing was, they proved the historians right. Scientists now believe that the early villages and the things found in the Fertile Crescent belong to a time many, many thousands of years ago.

LEARN MORE! READ THESE ARTICLES…
DAMASCUS, SYRIA (VOLUME 7)
ISRAEL (VOLUME 7)
NILE RIVER: EGYPT'S GIFT (VOLUME 8)

Answer: The Fertile Crescent was given its name for two reasons. First, it is crescent-shaped, like a New Moon. Second, it is an area that was very good for growing crops.

65

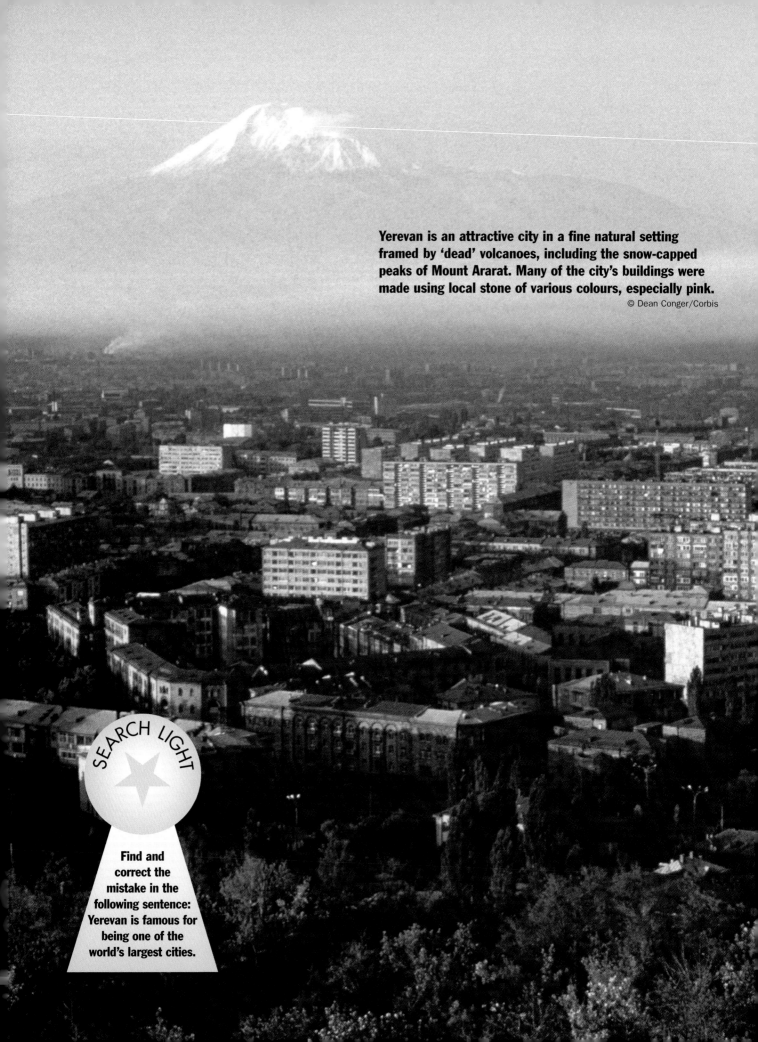

Yerevan is an attractive city in a fine natural setting framed by 'dead' volcanoes, including the snow-capped peaks of Mount Ararat. Many of the city's buildings were made using local stone of various colours, especially pink.

© Dean Conger/Corbis

SEARCH LIGHT

Find and correct the mistake in the following sentence: Yerevan is famous for being one of the world's largest cities.

City of Cafés

Yerevan is one of the world's oldest cities. A fortress was built there in 783 BC. Yerevan is the capital of Armenia, a country at the north-western edge of Asia. The Hrazdan River divides the city. In early times the city became an important stop for traders. In modern times dams have been built on the river to supply electric power for the city's many **industries**.

Yerevan

Republic Square lies at the centre of the city. Yerevan spreads out from the riverbank to the slopes of the surrounding hills. The peaks of Mount Aragats, Mount Azhdaak, and Mount Ararat can be seen from the city. All three are 'dead' volcanoes. Mount Ararat is traditionally considered the place where Noah's ark came to a rest at the end of the flood described in the Jewish and Christian Bible. Most of the houses in the city are pink because they are made with pink 'tuff' stones from the volcanoes.

Yerevan's many museums include the National Art Gallery and the Children's Art Gallery. There is also a painters' **bazaar** during weekends where paintings are sold at reasonable prices. The Matenadaran archives houses books that were written long ago. It has a wonderful collection of old illustrated **manuscripts**. The Erebuni Museum contains many historical objects, including coins and ancient tools.

One of the most unforgettable things about Yerevan is its many cafés. In summer there are so many outdoor cafés that it's often hard to tell where one ends and the next one begins!

LEARN MORE! READ THESE ARTICLES...
BIBLE (VOLUME 5) • ISTANBUL, TURKEY (VOLUME 7)
VOLCANOES (VOLUME 1)

DID YOU KNOW?
Many Armenians hold Mount Ararat sacred. They believe their ancestors were the first people to appear in the world - and therefore on the mountain - after the great flood described in the Bible.

Answer: Yerevan is famous for being one of the world's oldest cities.

67

City on Two Continents

Istanbul is the only city in the world that sits on two continents. It is divided by the Bosporus Strait - a narrow stretch of water that separates Europe from Asia. So part of Istanbul lies in Asia and part in Europe. The city has been a gateway between Asia and Europe for centuries. Today it is the largest city in Turkey and its most important port.

Istanbul has a long history. In the 7th century BC the Greeks built a **colony** on the site and called it Byzantium. For more than 1,000 years, beginning in the 4th century AD, the city was the capital of the Byzantine Empire. It became known as Constantinople during this period. In 1453 the Turks of the Ottoman Empire conquered Constantinople and made it their capital. After the fall of the Ottoman Empire, Turkey became a **republic** in 1923. The capital was then moved to Ankara. Istanbul took its current name in 1930.

Fires, earthquakes, and invasions have greatly damaged Istanbul over the years, but the old part of the city still has many historic sights. One of these is Topkapi Palace, where the Ottoman **sultans** lived. Another landmark is the Hagia Sophia, which was built as a church almost 1,500 years ago. It later became a **mosque** and is now a museum.

Of the many mosques built by the Ottomans, the Blue Mosque is the most famous. Another interesting place to visit is the Grand **Bazaar**. It has shops selling gold, carpets, **ceramics**, copper, brass, and hundreds of other items.

LEARN MORE! READ THESE ARTICLES...
ASIA (VOLUME 7) • EUROPE (VOLUME 6)
MEDITERRANEAN SEA (VOLUME 1)

The Hagia Sophia, in the background, and the Blue Mosque are two of the best-known sights in Istanbul.
© Danny Lehman/Corbis

Answer: b) Byzantium and Constantinople.

SEARCH LIGHT

Find and correct the mistake in the following sentence: Iran was once the centre of the mighty Ottoman Empire.

Modern Persia

The country of Iran, in south-western Asia, was the centre of a mighty empire in ancient times. Today it is a strict Islamic **republic**, meaning that its laws are based on the religion of Islam. Many people in the countries around Iran also follow Islam. However, most Iranians follow Shi'ah Islam, a form that is less common elsewhere. The country's capital is the ancient city of Tehran.

The people of the region have always called the land Iran, but outsiders gave it the name Persia. The name came from the province of Pars, or Persis, where some of the early kings of the region had their capital. In about 550 BC one of those kings, Cyrus the Great, expanded his kingdom and created the Persian Empire. The empire lasted for more than 200 years until the great Macedonian empire-builder Alexander the Great defeated the last Persian ruler. After that, the region changed hands many times.

All the different groups that ruled Iran through the centuries contributed to its rich culture. One of Iran's best-known poets was Omar Khayyam. He wrote beautiful poems that are still read today. Iran is also famous for its miniature paintings, silver work, and Persian rugs. Iran continues to produce these traditional crafts, but it has worked to develop modern **industries** as well.

Iran relies on selling its petroleum and natural gas for much of its income. The country also produces chemicals from those two substances. Iran borders the Persian Gulf and the Caspian Sea, and fisheries there provide jobs for some Iranians.

LEARN MORE! READ THESE ARTICLES...
DAMASCUS, SYRIA (VOLUME 7)
FROM THE *KALILAH WA DIMNAH*: THE POOR MAN AND THE
FLASK OF OIL (VOLUME 5) • ISLAM (VOLUME 5)

DID YOU KNOW?

The religion of Zoroastrianism was founded in Iran by a man named Zoroaster, or Zarathushtra, more than 2,500 years ago.

Shop windows in Tehran, Iran, display jewellery and other goods.
© Shepard Sherbell/Corbis

Answer: Iran was once the centre of the mighty Persian Empire.

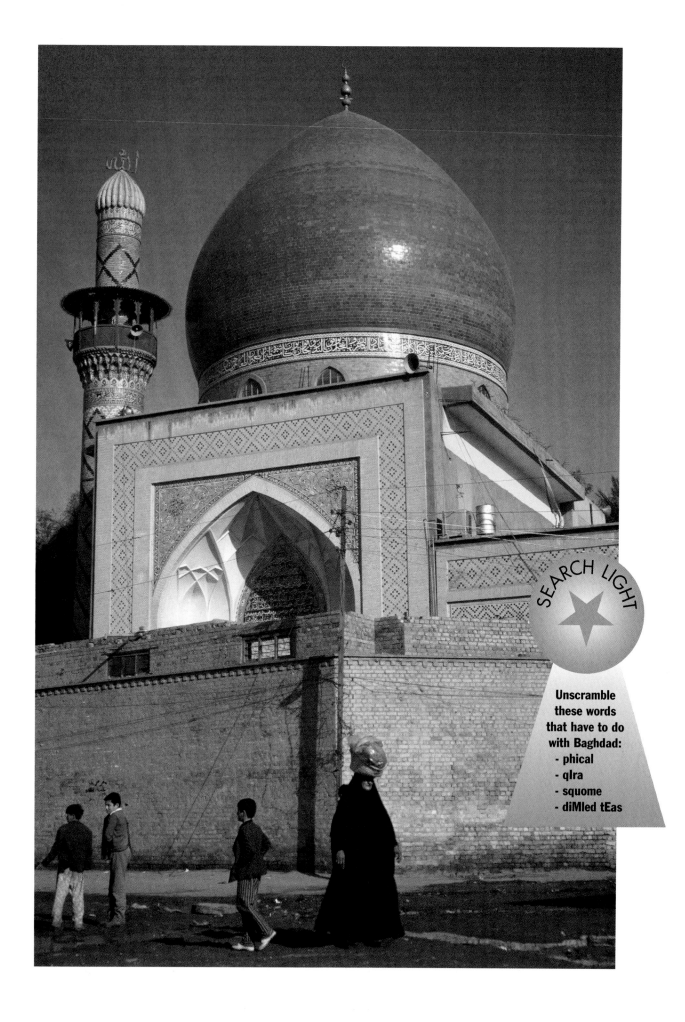

City of Arabian Nights

Have you heard the stories of *The Arabian Nights*? Did you know that most of the stories are set in Baghdad? Baghdad is the capital of Iraq. It lies on the banks of the Tigris River.

Baghdad

People have lived in the area where Baghdad now stands for about 4,000 years. The city itself, however, did not develop until many years later. About 1,200 years ago a Muslim caliph (leader) named al-Mansur chose a village called Baghdad for his capital. The new city was built within rounded walls. At the centre stood the caliph's palace and a grand **mosque**. People called Baghdad the City of Peace or the Round City. During the reign of a later caliph named Harun al-Rashid, Baghdad was said to be the richest and most beautiful city in the world. The stories in *The Arabian Nights* tell about the glory of Baghdad during this period.

Today Baghdad is one of the largest cities in the Middle East. It is also a centre of the art and culture of the religion of Islam. It has many mosques, museums, and libraries. People go to the Awqaf Library to study Arabic history and literature. The Iraqi National Museum has a famous collection of items from the country's early history.

Despite its many advantages, Baghdad has faced many problems in recent times. After Iraq invaded Kuwait in 1990, the United States and other countries bombed Baghdad and other parts of Iraq. Parts of the city were destroyed. Baghdad was damaged again in 2003, during another war with the United States. Once again the people of Baghdad had to work to rebuild their city.

LEARN MORE! READ THESE ARTICLES...
FERTILE CRESCENT (VOLUME 7)
ISLAM (VOLUME 5)
MYTHS AND LEGENDS, FOLKTALES AND FABLES
(VOLUME 5)

DID YOU KNOW?
The caliphs of Baghdad in the 800s and 900s AD were great supporters of the game of chess. The city was home to some of the world's best players.

Most of the people of Baghdad follow the religion of Islam. The city has many mosques, or houses of worship for Muslims.
© Charles & Josette Lenars/Corbis

Several cities were located on the shores of
Lake Tiberias in northern Israel in ancient times.
The lake is called the Sea of Galilee in the Bible.

SEARCH LIGHT

Fill in
the gap:
Israel's founding
as a Jewish state
caused problems
for the _____,
the Arab people
already living in
the same area.

The Jewish State

Jerusalem

Although Israel did not become a country until 1948, the region where it is located, formerly called Palestine, has a rich history. It was the ancient home of the Jewish people, and for many hundreds of years it has been home to Arabs. The region, especially the city of Jerusalem, is important to people of the Christian, Jewish, and Islamic faiths.

Much of Israel is a desert. But there are also well-watered areas where crops can grow. Israel's major crops are citrus fruits, flowers, and vegetables. An important feature of Israel is the Jordan River. It rises in the north and flows south into Lake Tiberias (the Sea of Galilee) and then into the Dead Sea, a large salt lake.

Israel was created as a country where Jews could rule themselves and live without fear of **persecution**. But this caused problems for the Arabs already living on the land. These people, called Palestinians, felt that the land was being taken away from them. The neighbouring Arab countries also objected to a Jewish state in Palestine and tried to overrun the country just after it was founded.

Israel won that war as well as several others. During one war Israel took control of areas called the Gaza Strip and the West Bank. Palestinians there want to form their own state. They also want control of part of Jerusalem, which Israel claims as its capital. The Israelis and the Palestinians have tried to settle their differences peacefully, but conflicts between the two groups continued into the 21st century.

LEARN MORE! READ THESE ARTICLES…
YASIR ARAFAT (VOLUME 4) • JUDAISM (VOLUME 5) • GOLDA MEIR (VOLUME 4)

DID YOU KNOW?
Salt water is buoyant - that is, it makes things float. The Dead Sea is so salty that when you swim in it, you float even if you don't want to.

Answer: Israel's founding as a Jewish state caused problems for the Palestinians, the Arab people already living in the same area.

Holy City

Jerusalem is a very holy city for Jews, Christians, and Muslims. The section of Jerusalem called the Old City is full of churches, **mosques**, and **synagogues**. People have lived in the Old City for nearly 5,000 years.

There are many sounds in the Old City. You can hear the ringing of church bells and the Muslim call to prayer from the **minarets**. You can also hear the sound of chanting at the Western Wall. The wall is the only remaining part of an ancient Jewish temple.

Jerusalem is holy to which three religions?
a) Islam, Buddhism, and Hinduism
b) Islam, Hinduism, and Judaism
c) Islam, Christianity, and Judaism

The Church of the Holy Sepulchre.
© Michael Nicholson/Corbis

Because of the sound of the prayers offered there, the wall is often called the Wailing Wall. Above it is the Temple Mount, which is sacred to Muslims. It is the site of the beautiful gold-capped **shrine** called the Dome of the Rock. It is said that Muhammad, the founder of Islam, made his journey to heaven from this site.

To the north of the Temple Mount lies Via Dolorosa, or Street of Sorrows. This is believed to be the path Jesus walked while carrying the cross. It ends at the Church of the Holy **Sepulchre**. This church is the most important shrine for Christians. It is said to have been built over the place where Jesus died, was buried, and rose from the dead.

Because of Jerusalem's religious importance, control of the city has long been disputed. Israel claims Jerusalem as its capital, but some people disagree with this claim. Among them is a group called the Palestinians, who live in East Jerusalem and nearby territories. Some of them want a separate state created for Palestinians, and they want part of Jerusalem to be its capital.

LEARN MORE! READ THESE ARTICLES…
CHRISTIANITY (VOLUME 5) • ISLAM (VOLUME 5) • JUDAISM (VOLUME 5)

Jews pray at the Western Wall. The Dome of the Rock is in the background.
© Richard T. Nowitz/Corbis

DID YOU KNOW?
Nearly 2,400 years ago the Egyptian king Ptolemy II Philadelphus took over the city of Amman. He decided to rename it. The name he chose? Philadelphia, for himself.

City on Seven Hills

Amman is the capital of the Hashemite Kingdom of Jordan. 'Hashemite' means that the ruling family is **descended** from the Prophet Muhammad. The city is spread over seven hills, called *jabal*s in the Arabic language. Most of Amman's historical sites are clustered in the downtown area, at the bottom of the *jabal*s.

Amman

An ancient **citadel** towers over the city of Amman. It is at the top of Al-Qala Hill. Al-Qasr is the most imposing building of the citadel. Al-Qasr means 'the palace'. Nearby is the Jordan Archaeological Museum. It has many exhibits from the **prehistoric** age up to recent times. Probably its most famous possessions are the Dead Sea Scrolls. These ancient **manuscripts** are about 2,000 years old, and they include parts of the Torah (the first five books of the Hebrew Bible) and other writings.

At the bottom of Al-Qala Hill is a Roman **amphitheatre**. The theatre was cut into the northern side of a hill and can seat 6,000 people. It is still used to stage shows, and it has two museums. The Jordan Folklore Museum has many things that tell us how the people of Jordan used to live. The Museum of Popular Traditions has traditional costumes and antique jewellery. Many of the costumes feature beautiful **embroidery**. The odeum is another theatre, nearly as old as the Roman one. It seats just 500 people. Romans used it as a concert hall, and it's still used for concerts.

Visitors to Amman enjoy the city's many bazaars (markets) called *souk*s. Each *souk* sells different things. The gold *souk* is greatly admired.

LEARN MORE! READ THESE ARTICLES...
FOLK ARTS AND CRAFTS (VOLUME 3) • JERUSALEM (VOLUME 7)
MUHAMMAD (VOLUME 5)

SEARCH LIGHT

In the Arabic language, *jabal* means
a) hill.
b) bazaar.
c) theatre.

Houses in Amman, Jordan, cover a hill above an ancient Roman amphitheatre. This huge outdoor theatre was built more than 1,800 years ago and is remarkably well preserved.
© Adam Woolfitt/Corbis

Answer: a) hill.

The City of Wells

Beirut, the capital of Lebanon, lies on the coast of the Mediterranean Sea. It is the country's chief port and largest city. Until the late 20th century, Beirut was a social and cultural centre of the Middle East. In many ways, the city was a complicated mix of peoples and ideas. People from all over the world have attended its schools, colleges, and universities, including the American University of Beirut.

Long ago the city was part of a region called Phoenicia. The Phoenicians called the city Be'erot, which means 'wells', because of its underground supply of water. It was one of the most attractive cities in the Middle East. For a long time Beirut was the most important port in the eastern Mediterranean. Its location made it a natural **crossroads** between Asia and Europe.

But Lebanon has been torn apart by many wars and conflicts. Much of Beirut was destroyed in a **civil war** that lasted from 1975 to 1991. Some parts of the city have been rebuilt now. Traditional two-story houses with red-tiled roofs sit side by side with fashionable new houses. Many houses and buildings, though, are still in bad shape and need to be repaired.

Despite the destruction, there are many things to see in Beirut. The American University of Beirut Museum, the Nicolas Sursock Museum, and the National Museum are some of them. At the National Museum you can see objects that are thousands of years old. The city also has many shopping centres and a large number of cafés where you can relax and enjoy Lebanese food, such as *baba ganouj* (aubergine dip) or *tabbouleh* (cracked-wheat salad).

SEARCH LIGHT

What event led to the destruction of large parts of the city of Beirut in the late 20th century?

LEARN MORE! READ THESE ARTICLES...
CEDARS (VOLUME 10) • AMMAN, JORDAN (VOLUME 7)
MEDITERRANEAN SEA (VOLUME 1)

A street vendor carries his goods on a bicycle through the streets of Beirut.
D. Mace/Robert Harding Picture Library

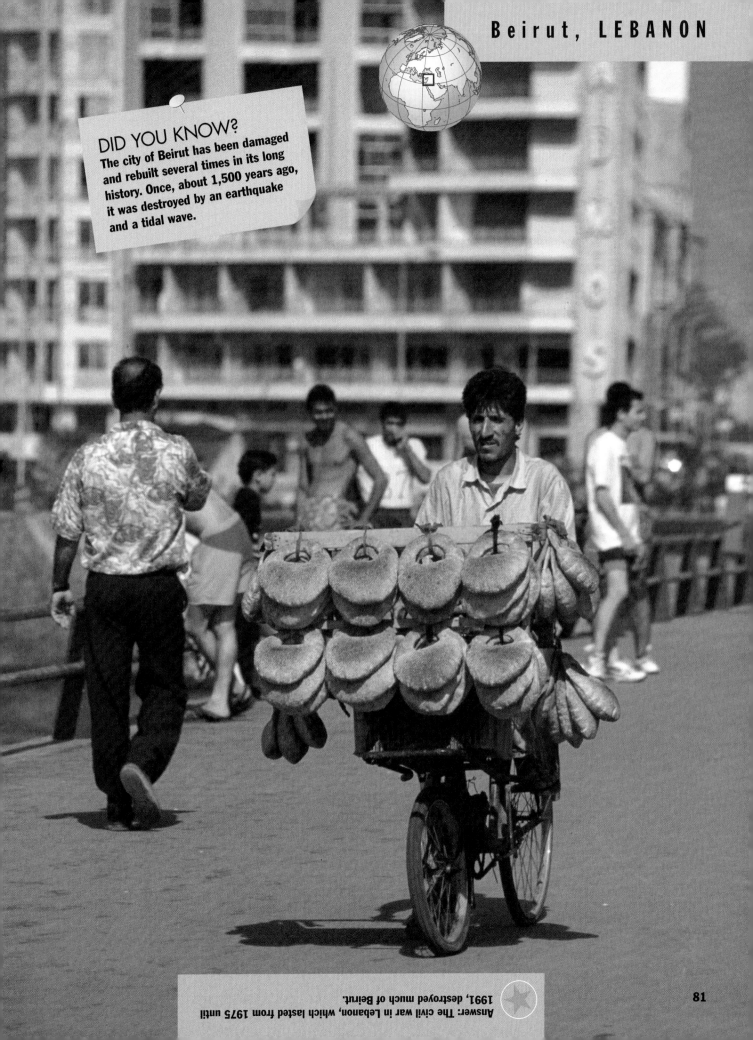

DID YOU KNOW?
The city of Beirut has been damaged and rebuilt several times in its long history. Once, about 1,500 years ago, it was destroyed by an earthquake and a tidal wave.

Answer: The civil war in Lebanon, which lasted from 1975 until 1991, destroyed much of Beirut.

Rocky Soils and Petroleum Riches

The sultanate of Oman is a country on the eastern coast of the Arabian **Peninsula** in south-western Asia. Oman's leader is called the sultan. He rules the country from a palace in Muscat, the capital city.

Oman is one of the hottest and driest countries in the world. Most of the country is rocky and sandy as well. Farming is possible only on narrow plains along the northern and southern coasts. The Al-Hajar Mountains separate the northern coastal plain, called Al-Batinah, from the vast desert to the south-west. The southern coastal plain lies in the region called Dhofar. Most of the country's people live on these **fertile** plains.

Dates are Oman's most important crop. Omani farmers also grow vegetables, bananas, mangoes, and melons. They water their crops through an ancient system of **canals**. The Dhofar region is well known for trees that produce the sweet-smelling substance called '**frankincense**'.

Fine camels are raised in the Dhofar region, where camel racing is a popular sport. Camels bred in Oman are among the best on the Arabian Peninsula. But the petroleum industry is the most important part of Oman's economy by far. Petroleum from Omani wells is sold to other countries and is made into petrol and other products.

DID YOU KNOW?

Frankincense comes from the oil of certain trees found only in Yemen, Somalia, and Oman. Merchants from these regions have traded in frankincense since ancient times, when the spice was considered important in worship and as a medicine.

Camel racing is a traditional sport in Oman.
© Arthur Thévenart/Corbis

Muscat

Omanis often gather for meals. If you were to join a typical group dinner, you'd probably have rice and spiced lamb or fish. Then you'd have dates for dessert and coffee or tea to drink. After the meal was over, the host might burn **incense**, probably the famous frankincense.

LEARN MORE! READ THESE ARTICLES...
DESERTS (VOLUME 1) • IRAN (VOLUME 7) • OIL (VOLUME 2)

SEARCH LIGHT

Fill in the gaps: Oman is one of the _____ and _____ countries in the world, with little yearly rainfall.

Answer: Oman is one of the hottest and driest countries in the world, with little yearly rainfall.

Holiest City of Islam

Mecca is the holiest city for followers of the religion of Islam. The city, located in Saudi Arabia, is the birthplace of the Prophet Muhammad, the founder of Islam. Muslims all over the world face in the direction of Mecca five times each day to pray.

Fill in the gaps: Muslims go to Mecca to see the birthplace of the _____ _____.

The Haram, or Great Mosque, and the Kaaba are the most important places in Mecca. The **mosque** is said to be a copy of God's house in heaven. It can hold a million worshippers. The Kaaba lies in the central courtyard of the mosque. It is a cube-shaped **shrine** made of black stone and wood. This is the holiest shrine of Islam. It is the object toward which Muslims pray when facing Mecca, and it is the most important site for Muslim **pilgrims** to visit when they go to the city. Muslims call the pilgrimage, or journey, to Mecca the *hajj*. All adult Muslims are supposed to try to make the trip at least once.

There are numerous sites from Islamic history in Mecca. Mount Hira, in the north-eastern part of the city, has a cave where Muhammad went to **meditate** in private before he became a **prophet**. Muslims believe he received the first verse of the Koran, the holy book of Islam, in this cave.

Mecca changed greatly in the 20th century. The areas surrounding the Great Mosque were cleared. New houses were built. The streets were made wider, and new tunnels were built to handle more traffic. Like Riyadh (the nation's capital), Mecca is now one of the largest and most modern cities in Saudi Arabia.

LEARN MORE! READ THESE ARTICLES...
AMMAN, JORDAN (VOLUME 7)
MUHAMMAD (VOLUME 5) • VATICAN CITY (VOLUME 6)

Mecca — Riyadh ★

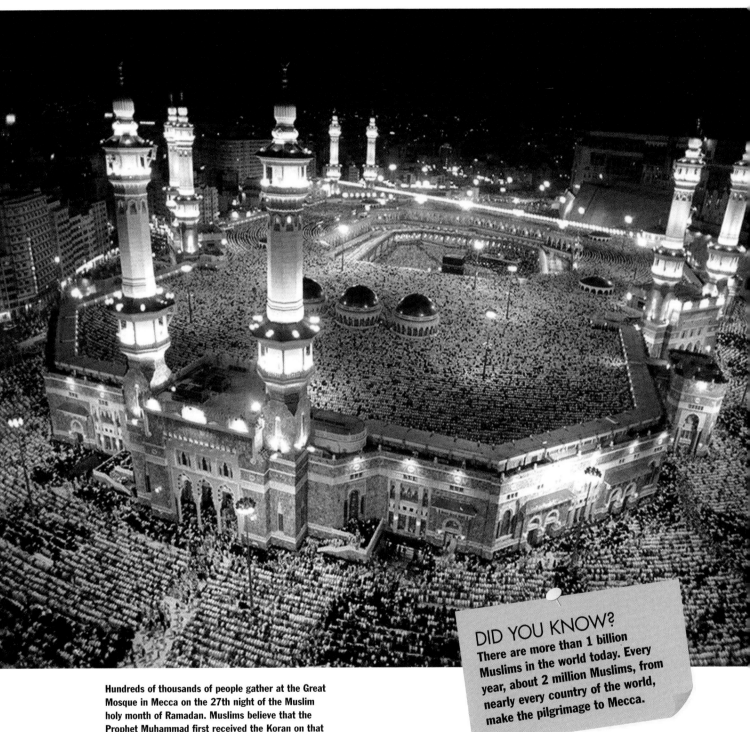

Hundreds of thousands of people gather at the Great Mosque in Mecca on the 27th night of the Muslim holy month of Ramadan. Muslims believe that the Prophet Muhammad first received the Koran on that night many years ago.

© AFP/Corbis

DID YOU KNOW?

There are more than 1 billion Muslims in the world today. Every year, about 2 million Muslims, from nearly every country of the world, make the pilgrimage to Mecca.

Answer: Muslims go to Mecca to see the birthplace of the Prophet Muhammad.

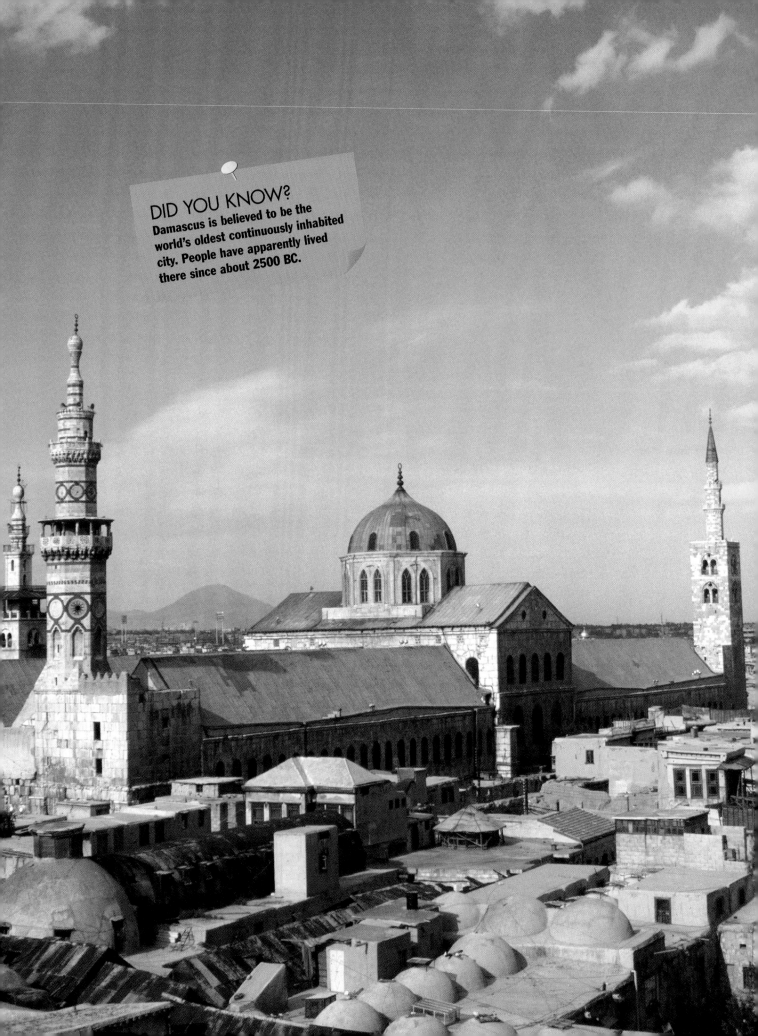

DID YOU KNOW?
Damascus is believed to be the world's oldest continuously inhabited city. People have apparently lived there since about 2500 BC.

Pearl of the East

Damascus is the capital of Syria and one of the oldest cities in the world. Travellers who visited Damascus in the past wrote about its many trees, its olive groves, and its streams and fountains. Some of these parks and gardens still exist. And for this reason people still call Damascus the 'Pearl of the East'.

In the old part of Damascus, many people live very much as people did hundreds of years ago. Most of them still live in small single-storey houses built close together. Rising above them are the graceful minarets (towers) and domes of the city's many **mosques**, where believers in the religion of Islam worship. The Great Mosque of Damascus is the oldest surviving stone mosque in the world.

One of the most colourful areas of Damascus is the region of the khans and **bazaars**. Long ago khans were trade, storage, and resting places for camel **caravans**. The Khan Asa'ad Pasha is a beautiful building. It has a striking gate and a black-and-white marble top supported by marble pillars. It is still a centre of trade. The bazaars are lined with shops, stalls, and cafés. They're filled with the noise of people bargaining for the best deal.

Many streets in the bazaar were once devoted to particular trades. You could find the Street of the Saddlers, Street of the Slipper Merchants, and Street of the Water-Pipe Makers. You could also find the Street of the Spice Men, Street of the Dyers, and many others. The longest and busiest of them all was the famous Street Called Straight. It is mentioned in the Bible.

LEARN MORE! READ THESE ARTICLES…
AMMAN, JORDAN (VOLUME 7) • CAMELS (VOLUME 12) • ISLAM (VOLUME 5)

SEARCH LIGHT

Why would the streets in the Damascus bazaars have names like the Street of the Spice Men?

The minarets, or towers, of the Ommayed Mosque rise above the surrounding buildings in Damascus, Syria.
© Charles & Josette Lenars/Corbis

Answer: Having the streets named after what was sold there made it easier for shoppers to find what they were looking for.

87

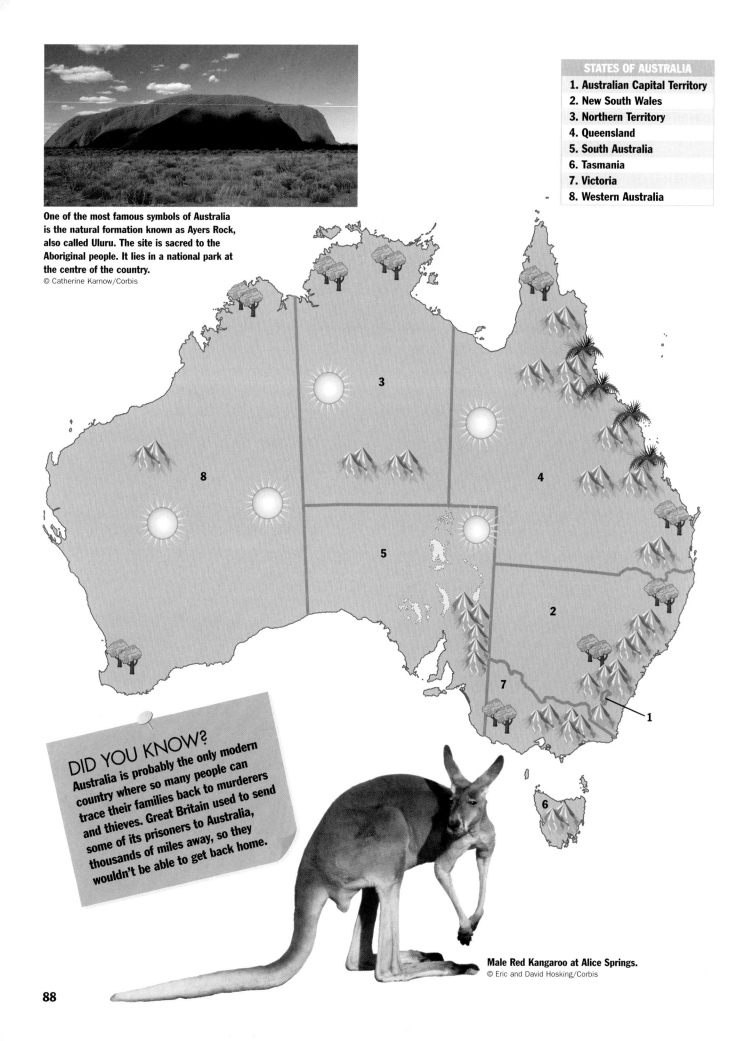

One of the most famous symbols of Australia is the natural formation known as Ayers Rock, also called Uluru. The site is sacred to the Aboriginal people. It lies in a national park at the centre of the country.
© Catherine Karnow/Corbis

DID YOU KNOW?
Australia is probably the only modern country where so many people can trace their families back to murderers and thieves. Great Britain used to send some of its prisoners to Australia, thousands of miles away, so they wouldn't be able to get back home.

Male Red Kangaroo at Alice Springs.
© Eric and David Hosking/Corbis

Island Continent

The island continent of Australia lies between the Indian and Pacific oceans. Australia is the smallest, flattest, and driest continent. And it has fewer people than other **inhabited** continents. Australia is both a continent and a country, and the map shows you the country's states.

Find and correct the mistake in the following sentence: Australia has many animals that are not found anywhere else in the world. Two well-known ones are the buffalo and the spider.

Australia can be divided into three major parts. The Western **Plateau** covers most of the continent. It gets little rainfall except in its south-west corner. But great forests do grow there. Elsewhere on the plateau, wells are the only way to get water. The Eastern Uplands run along the east coast. And the Interior Lowlands lie in between. There you'll find the colourful 335-metre-tall Ayers Rock, also called by its Aboriginal name, Uluru.

More than half of the country has been turned into pastures for animals, mostly sheep. Australia has the largest number of sheep in the world and produces more wool than any other country. Australia also has many animals that are not found anywhere else in the world. Two well-known examples are the koala and the kangaroo. The duck-billed platypus and the echidna are two unusual egg-laying mammals.

Many visitors go diving along Australia's Great Barrier Reef, the largest coral **reef** in the world. It stretches for miles and has an amazing display of fish. However, scientists are worried that the reef may be damaged if world climate changes cause the temperature of the sea to rise.

Australians are often called 'Aussies', and most are of European **heritage**. But there is also a large native Aboriginal population. Most Aboriginals live outside the cities in the inner part of the country called the Outback. Today the Aboriginals make boomerangs to sell to tourists, although they originally used them for hunting.

LEARN MORE! READ THESE ARTICLES…
CORAL (VOLUME 11) • GREAT BARRIER REEF (VOLUME 7)
KATH WALKER (VOLUME 3)

Answer: Australia has many animals that are not found anywhere else in the world. Two well-known ones are the koala and the kangaroo.

89

DID YOU KNOW?
Canberra was a planned city - that is,
it was all built at once according to
an architect's design. A man named
Walter Burley Griffin won the
government's contest to see who
would design the city. He named
Canberra's Lake Burley Griffin after
himself.

Meeting Place On a Hill

Canberra is the capital of Australia. Long ago it was just a small settlement called Canberry. The name was later changed to Canberra, which means 'meeting place'.

Canberra lies in a plain at the foot of the Australian Alps in southeastern Australia. The city spreads out on both sides of the Molonglo River.

Aboriginal chalk drawing in front of the Old Parliament House in Canberra.
© Liba Taylor/Corbis

The new **Parliament** House is built into the Capital Hill, the main hill in the city. Its roof is lined with grass so that it appears to blend into the landscape. Inside the Parliament House there are nearly 3,000 works by Australian artists on display.

The Old Parliament House is farther down the hill. It's now the home of the National Portrait Gallery. Another interesting museum is the National Gallery of Australia. It contains traditional **Aboriginal** (native Australian) art as well as paintings from different parts of the world. Sculptures, drawings, photographs, furniture, pottery, **textiles**, and silverwork are also on display.

The Questacon near the National Gallery is a science museum for children. Its five **galleries** have more than 200 gadgets that demonstrate natural events and objects. For example, you can find out firsthand what an earthquake feels like.

The National Botanic Gardens are located on the lower slopes of Black Mountain. Here you can see some of the most interesting Australian plants. There's an area that has plants used by the Aboriginals. There are also a rainforest area and a eucalyptus lawn. The lawn has 600 different kinds of eucalyptus tree. Some of these trees grow almost 92 metres tall! Near the city is Namadgi National Park, which is popular with mountain climbers.

LEARN MORE! READ THESE ARTICLES...
AUSTRALIA (VOLUME 7) • EUCALYPTUS (VOLUME 10)
CATHY FREEMAN (VOLUME 4)

SEARCH LIGHT

What is special about the roof of the new Parliament House in Canberra?

This painting of the tree of life, by David Malangi, was done on tree bark. It is one of the many artworks by Aboriginal (native Australian) artists on display at the National Gallery of Australia, at Canberra.
© Penny Tweedie/Corbis

Island of Reefs
Within Reefs

The Great **Barrier** Reef is one of the great natural wonders of the world. It is actually a system of many individual reefs and islets (small islands). Altogether there are 2,100 individual reefs in the Great Barrier Reef. This huge ridge of coral reefs is separated from land by a **channel** of water 48 kilometres wide.

The Great Barrier Reef was formed over millions of years from mounds of coral. A coral is a soft animal that supports its body inside a hard hollow shell. When the coral died, its shell remained and other corals grew on top of it. Over those millions of years, the corals remained hardened and became cemented together. Slowly they were covered with underwater plants, **debris** from the ocean, and other corals.

Exploring the Great Barrier Reef at low tide.
© Staffan Widstrand/Corbis

The Great Barrier Reef lies in the Pacific Ocean off the coast of Queensland in north-eastern Australia. From north to south its length is equal to the entire Pacific Coast of the United States - extending more than 2,000 kilometres! The water is so clear and pollution-free at the Great Barrier Reef that people can glimpse the wonderful **marine** life deep underwater.

Besides the 400 types of coral, there are such animals as anemones, snails, lobsters, prawns, jellyfish, giant clams, and dugongs. And there are more than 1,500 **species** of saltwater fish. Many of the small fish have brilliant colours and unusual shapes.

The Great Barrier Reef was named a World Heritage site in 1981.

LEARN MORE! READ THESE ARTICLES...
CORAL (VOLUME 11) • ISLANDS (VOLUME 1) • SEAWEED (VOLUME 10)

SEARCH LIGHT

True or false? The Great Barrier Reef is made of rock.

From north to south, the length of Australia's Great Barrier Reef is equal to that of the entire Pacific Coast of the United States!
© Australian Picture Library/Corbis

DID YOU KNOW?

Though it isn't truly a single structure, the 350,000-square-kilometre Great Barrier Reef is often referred to as the largest structure ever built by living things. And people had no hand in it!

A Magnificent Harbour City

Sydney is Australia's largest city and one of the most important ports in the South Pacific Ocean. It's also the capital of the state of New South Wales. Sydney is built on low hills surrounding a wonderful harbour on Australia's south-eastern coast. Its beaches are very popular, especially for surfing. And in 2000 the city hosted the Summer Olympic Games.

Sydney Cove is the small sheltered inlet where Australia's first permanent European settlement began. It used to be Sydney's shipping centre, and its old landing place (or quay) is now a tourist centre called Circular Quay. The quay has many walkways, cafés, parks, and docks for the ferries that crisscross the harbour. The nearby Sydney Opera House has a glittering white roof that looks like seashells. Besides opera, the Opera House presents plays, classical music concerts, ballets, and films. Darling Harbour just west of downtown has an aquarium, museums, and gardens.

Sydney Harbour Bridge and The Rocks, a historic district in Sydney.
© Royalty-Free/Corbis

The oldest part of Sydney is called The Rocks. This historic district has **cobbled** streets lined with houses that were built by the first British settlers. The Rocks draws crowds of shoppers during the weekend market and has many galleries selling arts and crafts. Here you'll also find the Museum of Contemporary Art.

Macquarie Street is known for its early public buildings. The street is named after the governor who had them built. Landmarks include the **Parliament** House, Sydney Hospital, the Mint Building (which used to produce money), and the beautiful Hyde Park Barracks (which used to house soldiers). Nearby, the large grassy field called the Domain, which was once set aside for public ceremonies, today provides a place for lunchtime sports and candlelight Christmas caroling.

LEARN MORE! READ THESE ARTICLES...
CANBERRA, AUSTRALIA (VOLUME 7) • OPERA (VOLUME 3) • WAVES (VOLUME 1)

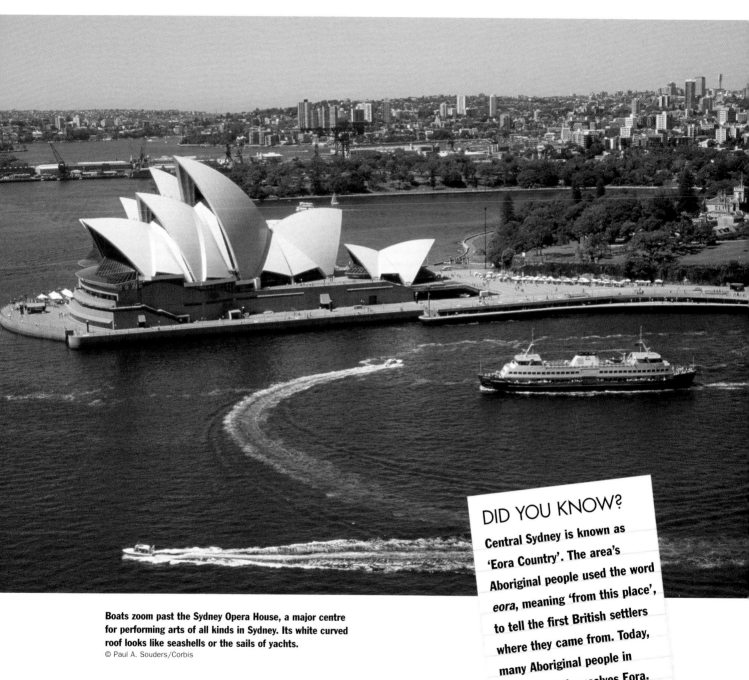

Boats zoom past the Sydney Opera House, a major centre for performing arts of all kinds in Sydney. Its white curved roof looks like seashells or the sails of yachts.
© Paul A. Souders/Corbis

DID YOU KNOW?

Central Sydney is known as 'Eora Country'. The area's Aboriginal people used the word *eora*, meaning 'from this place', to tell the first British settlers where they came from. Today, many Aboriginal people in Sydney call themselves Eora.

Answer: a) the capital of New South Wales and Australia's largest city.

95

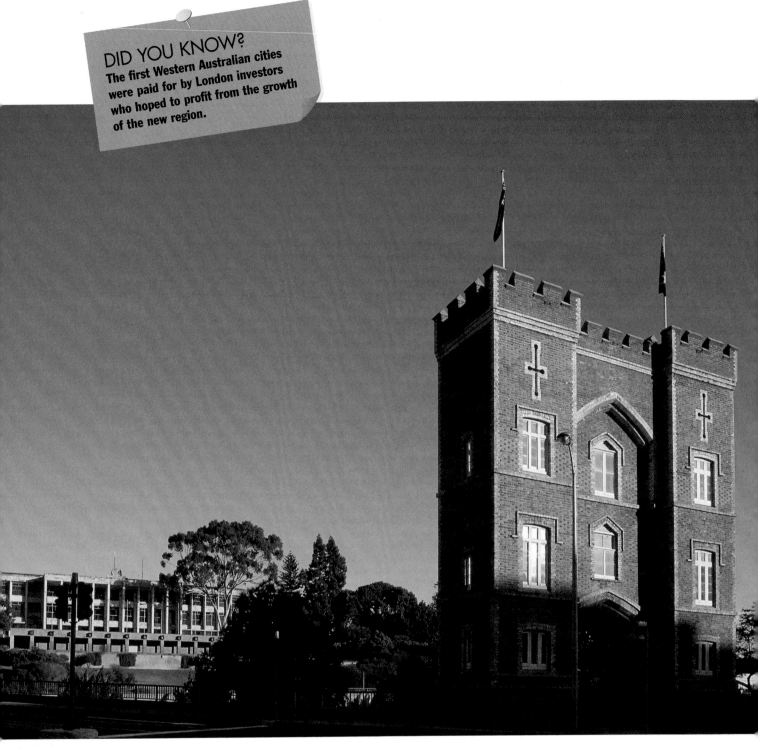

The Parliament House (left) in Perth is where the legislature of Western Australia meets. The Barracks Arch (right) is all that's left of a building that once housed British soldiers who guarded the jail.
© Paul A. Souders/Corbis

Desert State

SEARCH LIGHT

Find and correct the mistake in the following sentence: Many of Perth's roads and buildings were built by Canadians.

Western Australia is Australia's largest state. Much of it is desert. It receives little rainfall and the temperature is often higher than 38°C. Most of its people live in Perth, a coastal city that is the state capital.

The first people to live in Western Australia moved there at least 40,000 years ago. These **Aboriginal** people probably came from islands in Southeast Asia. As they continued to

Traditional Aboriginal (native Australian) face painting.
© Penny Tweedie/Corbis

arrive, they probably introduced to Australia the wild dog called the 'dingo'.

The first Europeans to see Western Australia may have been Portuguese sailors in the 1520s. But they didn't land. The Dutch East India Company, a trading company, sailed into the Indian Ocean in the early 1600s. The Dutch mapped the coastline, but they didn't stay either.

In 1829 Captain James Stirling of the British Navy started the first permanent European settlement in Australia at what is now Perth. Before then, the only Europeans living in Australia had been British **convicts** sent there by the British government. About 4,000 settlers joined Captain Stirling in the new **colony**.

Because of difficult living conditions, many of the settlers died over the next few years. But things gradually improved, and by 1835 the settlers were able to feed themselves. During the 1850s and 1860s, the British forced male convicts to construct many of the colony's roads and public buildings.

Western Australia became a state in 1901. From the 1940s through the 1960s, its population doubled. Today the state is home to about 2 million people, and Perth has one of the highest populations of Australia's cities.

LEARN MORE! READ THESE ARTICLES...
AUSTRALIA (VOLUME 7)
CANBERRA, AUSTRALIA (VOLUME 7) • DESERTS (VOLUME 1)

Land of the Long White Cloud

New Zealand is an island country in the South Pacific Ocean. Though it looks close to Australia on maps, the two countries are actually more than 1,600 kilometres apart. New Zealand has two main islands, called North and South Island. Cook **Strait**, a narrow stretch of sea, separates the two. Wellington, the capital city, is on North Island. It lies farther south than any other national capital in the world. New Zealand's largest city, Auckland, is also on North Island.

Both islands have mountains and hills. The Southern Alps is a long chain of mountains on South Island. The mountains trap the moist ocean air, and they are often wrapped in clouds. The first people to live in New Zealand, the Maori, called the country Aotearoa, meaning 'land of the long white cloud'.

New Zealand is known for Merino sheep, which are famous for their wool. Huge sheep ranches are scattered among the hills on South Island. New Zealand also produces excellent butter, cheese, and meat.

New Zealand has unique wildlife. The long-beaked kiwi, a bird that cannot fly, is found only in New Zealand. The bird is one of the country's national symbols - and New Zealanders themselves are sometimes even called Kiwis.

Traditional Maori culture has survived, but now it's blended with the European culture of modern New Zealand. You can still hear traditional Maori music played on the flute and see traditional Maori dances. Wood carving, painting, and making things of woven **flax** are Maori crafts.

Wellington

LEARN MORE! READ THESE ARTICLES...
KIWIS (VOLUME 11) • KIRI TE KANAWA (VOLUME 3)
WELLINGTON (VOLUME 7)

DID YOU KNOW?
New Zealand is home to a place with one of the longest names in the world, a hill called Taumatawhaka-tangihangakoauauotamateaturipukaka-pikimaungahoronukupokaiwhenua-kitanatahu.

A gondola car rides high above the harbour at Queenstown, New Zealand.
© Royalty-Free/Corbis

Answer: Long before Europeans arrived in New Zealand, the islands were inhabited by the Maori. The Maori came to New Zealand from the group of islands called Polynesia.

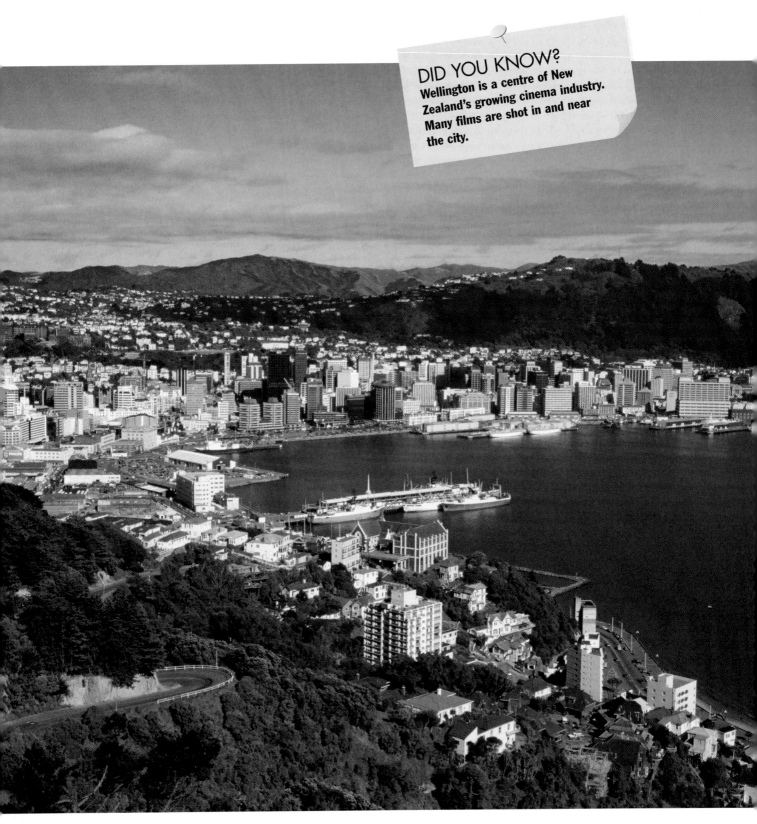

Green hills surround the city of Wellington.
Its harbour serves as a major port for New Zealand.
© Dallas and John Heaton/Corbis

A Visit to New Zealand's Capital

Wellington is the capital of New Zealand, an island country near Australia. It lies on the shores and green hills surrounding a beautiful bay. The city's centre is called Civic Square. It is made up of a group of buildings with an open square in the middle. The buildings include the National Library, the City Gallery, and Capital Discovery Place - a science and **technology** museum for children.

From Civic Square, you can reach Lambton Harbour by going across the City-to-Sea Bridge. The bridge is decorated with carvings and lovely artwork - all of it created by Maori artists. The Maori are the original people of New Zealand. From the street named Lambton **Quay**, visitors often take a cable car to reach the **botanical** gardens located in the hills above Wellington. The cable car ride provides some of the best views of the city.

The botanical gardens have many trees and plants not seen elsewhere. They also have many varieties of roses on display. The Bolton Memorial

Botanical gardens in Wellington, New Zealand.
© Paul A. Souders/Corbis

Park, a burial site for some of Wellington's first settlers, is located within the gardens. Along a section of the city's shoreline is the Oriental Parade. It is a beautiful place that is often crowded with joggers, cyclists, sunbathers, and swimmers. Many people swim out to the large fountain anchored offshore.

Wellington is home to the National Museum of New Zealand (Te Papa Tongarewa). Also popular is the Colonial Cottage Museum, the family home of Katherine Mansfield, one of New Zealand's most famous authors.

LEARN MORE! READ THESE ARTICLES...
CANBERRA, AUSTRALIA (VOLUME 7)
NEW ZEALAND (VOLUME 7) • ROSES (VOLUME 10)

G L O S S A R Y

abominable horrible or disgusting

Aboriginal relating to the original people to live in an area; *especially*, the original peoples of Australia

acid a chemical substance, often producing a burning effect when it interacts with another material

altar raised place on which sacrifices are offered or religious ceremonies are performed

amphitheatre building with seats rising in curved rows around an open space where games and plays take place

archaeologist person who studies past human life as shown by the tools, buildings, and other objects left by ancient peoples

architect person who designs and plans buildings and oversees their construction

architecture the art of designing and building structures, especially buildings that can be lived and worked in

autonomous independent and self-governing

barrier object or structure that blocks the ability to reach another object or place

basin the area of land drained by a river and its branches

bazaar marketplace where many kinds of goods are sold; *especially*, such a marketplace in Asia or Africa

botanical (noun: botany) having to do with plant life

canal artificial waterway for boats or for draining or supplying water to land

caravan group of pack animals or of vehicles travelling together one behind the other

cathedral large church where a bishop is in charge

ceramics objects made out of clay baked at high temperatures

channel narrow passageway between two areas of water

citadel castle or fortress that protects a city

civil war war between opposing groups of citizens of the same country or nation

climate average weather in a particular area

cobbled made of rounded stones larger than a pebble and smaller than a boulder

colony (adjective: colonial; verb: colonize) settlement established in a distant territory and controlled by a more powerful and expanding nation

communism (adjective: communist) system of government in which all property is owned by the state or community and all citizens are supposed to have a share in the total wealth

convict (noun) person serving a prison sentence

crossroads place where roads cross; also, a central meeting place or a decision-making point

cuisine style of cooking; also, foods made in that style

customhouse place where duties or taxes are paid on goods coming into or leaving a country

debris rubbish or fragments

delta large triangular area made of material deposited at the mouth of a river, where it empties into the sea

descended (adjective) related through a long line of ancestors

duct pipe, tube, or channel through which liquid or gases flow

dynasty series of rulers of the same family

embroidery needlework done to decorate cloth

emperor (feminine: empress) the ruler of an empire

export something that is carried or sent abroad, especially for sale in another country

extinct no longer existing

fertile rich and productive; able to yield quality crops in large quantities

flax the fibre from which linen cloth is made

frankincense a sweet-smelling substance from an African or Arabian tree

gallery room or building that is used to display special objects or works of art

glacier large river-like body of ice moving slowly down a slope or spreading over a land surface

handicrafts articles, such as pottery, made by hand by an individual person

heritage background or descent

humidity (adjective: humid) moisture or dampness; *especially*, the amount of moisture in the air

incense substance that produces a sweet smell when burned

industry business and manufacturing

inhabited (adjective) occupied; having residents

inlaid decorated with materials set into the surface

legislature an organized government group with the power to make laws

loot to steal from a home or public place, especially during rioting or wartime

mangrove tropical tree or shrub that has partly exposed roots and grows thickly in areas of salty water

manuscript handwritten or typewritten document

marine having to do with the ocean

mausoleum large or fancy tomb

meditation (verb: meditate) quiet focussed concentration, meant to calm and clear the mind; sometimes used to reach a spiritual awareness

minaret in Islamic architecture, the tall slender tower of a mosque, from which Muslims are called to prayer

monastery housing for people who have taken religious vows, especially for monks

monk man who lives apart from society, either alone or in a community of men, so that he can devote all his time to religious life

monsoon regular period of heavy rainfall and wind, especially in southern Asia

mosque Muslim place of worship

native (adjective) living or growing naturally in a particular region

natural resources the materials or qualities supplied by nature (such as minerals or water power) that make a place valuable to people, usually for industrial and manufacturing purposes

pagoda tower-like Asian temple or memorial building several storeys tall, with the edges of the roof at each level curving upwards

parliament the law-making body of some governments

peninsula finger of land with water on three sides

persecution cruel or harmful treatment for an extended period of time, often due to one's beliefs

pilgrim person who travels to a shrine or holy place to worship

pilgrimage journey made to a holy place to worship there

plateau wide land area with a fairly level surface raised sharply above the land on at least one side

plaza open place or area formed at the meeting of two or more streets

prehistoric having to do with times before written history

procession group of people moving along in an orderly, often ceremonial way

prophet holy person who acts as a messenger between God and people; also, a gifted person with the ability to correctly predict future events

quay structure built along the bank of a waterway for use as a landing place

reef raised length of rocks, coral, or sand at or near the surface of water

region general area; also, a specific district

regional characteristic of a particular area

republic form of government in which citizens who are allowed to vote elect officials and representatives responsible for governing by law

seclusion isolation or separation from others

secretariat a department that handles an international or government organization

sepulchre place of burial

shrine place where honour or worship is offered to a saint or deity

species group of living things that have certain characteristics in common and share a name

steppe land that is dry, usually rather level, and covered with grass

strait narrow channel connecting two large bodies of water

sultan king or ruler, especially of a Muslim state

synagogue Jewish house of worship

tableland broad flat area of high land

technology scientific ideas and knowledge put to actual use in actions, machines, and processes

temple building used for worship

text written work

textile cloth

typhoon major tropical storm that occurs in the Pacific Ocean and features high winds moving in circular patterns; in the Atlantic Ocean such storms are called 'hurricanes'

wildlife sanctuary place of protection for animals and plants